David
love

best wishes
xxx

Speaking for Myself

An Autobiography
by
Lynda Gallilee

Published by
RIFTSWOOD PUBLISHING

First Published in Great Britain 2004
by
RIFTSWOOD PUBLISHING
40 Willow Drive, Normanby, Middlesbrough, Cleveland. TS6 0HP

Printed by
REDPRESS
14 Queen Street, Redcar,
Cleveland. TS10 1AE

ISBN
0-9548500-1-7

CONTENTS

Dedicated to my Mam and late Dad

SPEAKING FOR MYSELF

By

Lynda Gallilee.

This autobiography is simply my way of inviting you to take my hand and share with me, the eventful journey of my life. A journey which hasn't been particularly dangerous or adventurous, since I haven't trekked across any deserts or scaled any mountains, but still, it's a journey that I hope you will enjoy.

Along the way there will be no short cuts, no piggy-back rides and very few resting places, in fact I can tell you now that our journey will be uphill all the way, but we both know don't we that the steeper the climb, the lovelier the view, and from where I'm standing I can assure you that the view is truly magnificent.

Admittedly the road ahead will be stony in places. Society has already marked out the 'No Go' areas and more often than not it will try to dictate our way. Yet if we stay resolute in our direction and attune our ears to the Lord's voice, then I'm certain that with His guidance and our perseverance, we will eventually find our way home.

During our time together I promise to lead you down pathways you've never dreamt existed, and show you secret avenues where only I have walked, and at every corner and crossroad, as we pause to catch our breath, I'll share with you the many memories I have about the various roads which we are about to travel. Some roads will be misty with teardrops and other roads will echo with laughter but one thing I'm sure of, at the end of our journey, you and I will emerge into the sunshine as friends.

The way I see it I began my life with an extra package in my knapsack. One that I can never shed and one which no one else can shoulder for me. I'll never know why I was the one chosen to carry it but I realised a long long time ago that I have no alternative but to carry it every step of the way.

To compensate for this weighty package the Lord has provided me with many gifts and as time goes by, and we get to know one another better, I promise that I will tell you about them all in detail. Shall I give you a few clues? Well first of all He gave me a pair of stout walking boots in the shape of my Mum and Dad. Wonderful strong people who kept hold of my hands until I struggled to my feet and who then led me out onto the right path and pointed the way forward.

Then at various milestones along the way He has dotted the odd friend to inspire me. Truly remarkable people who have whispered words of encouragement into my ear whenever pain and exhaustion has threatened to cloud my vision.

And it was just when I was getting used to travelling alone, that the Lord, in His goodness, conjured up for me a loving companion – an extra special person to walk life's journey with me and since we've been together, He's heaped on us both as many blessings as our arms could carry.

Some time ago I found that deep deep in the folds of my knapsack that the Lord had tucked away His most precious gift of all – the tiny parcel of faith - and I suppose this is really what my story is all about. I'd like to take this parcel of faith and share it with you, and who knows, maybe together we can scatter the seeds of Christianity wherever they should fall.

I must tell you that this story wasn't written on impulse. It's a story that's been simply biding its time, just waiting to be told. All credit for the work must go to the Lord who created me, because after all, I am merely His advocate. It was He who formulated the words on the pages and who planted each bright new idea in my mind. So come, take my hand my friend, we have a long and difficult road in front of us.

BEST FOOT FORWARD

I have to smile to myself whenever I hear people talking about the 'quality' of life and how much it matters, and I wonder, if they ever stop to consider the fact that some of us in society have had very little choice in the matter? We've simply learnt to be satisfied with the kind of life that we have been given.

Yet how grateful I am that my Mam struggled and screamed to give birth to me on that October night, more than fifty years ago.

It goes without saying that Mam and Dad were terribly down-hearted when they were told of my cerebral palsy, but the world didn't suddenly stop turning for them, it just tilted a little, giving their eyes a whole new perspective and from that day on they decided that instead of hiding me away in some corner, they would ease me out gently into society and encourage me to play my part.

Being born disabled isn't a major catastrophe you know, neither is it a bundle of laughs – let us just say it's an inconvenience.

Life for me is one continuous struggle, from waking up in the morning, to that delicious moment when I lay my head on the pillow each night. I drift off to sleep, always thankful for the day that has passed, always eager for tomorrow. Oh, yes, I love life with an intensity which hurts and I try to live it to the full, even though I'm bound and gagged in a body which restricts and humiliates me. A body which mocks my intellect and scoffs at my capabilities. Yet so varied are my days, so happy are my days, I wouldn't change places with anyone.

In my book, life isn't merely about survival. It's about giving the best of myself to everyone that I meet. It's about striving for goals that seem way out of reach and then being pleasantly surprised to discover just how close they really are.

It's about realising the things that I can do and forgetting about those that I can't. To me life's about taking punch after punch and still coming back for more. And believe me when you're disabled the punches come more frequently and the bruising is internal.

In my opinion, life should never be denied to a disabled child. Any heart that beats deserves to be loved, any lips that smile deserve to be kissed, and any outstretched arms deserve to be embraced. The disabled children throughout this world must be allowed to grow and blossom just like the flowers in the meadows, because just like the flowers, these children have their own valuable contributions to make.

Sometimes, in moments of prayerfulness, I wonder whether I have been given this gift of writing as some sort of apology for my disability – no apology was necessary – I wouldn't have missed all this happiness for the world. And if I had to choose between being born strong and healthy and being parted from my childlike faith, then believe me, I would rather much stay as I am.

Before putting our best foot forward, perhaps I should take a little time to introduce myself to you... My name is Lynda... Wait a minute, I've had a better idea! Why don't we sit for a few moments within the quietness of this chapel porch, and then if you would like me to, I'll tell you the story of my uncertain beginning? After all, this was the church where my Mam and Dad were married, so what better place could there be for our journey to begin.

Sometimes I wonder which situation is the most frustrating –

being born with a disability or being the parent of a disabled child. It has always been my Mam's belief that 'special' people are chosen to be these parents, and I have good reason to agree with her because the Lord chose exactly the right couple to be my Mam and Dad.

For twenty-nine long agonising hours Mam laboured to give me life and being her first child I suppose neither she nor Dad had any idea about the serious complications which were occurring as the minutes and hours ticked slowly by.

Up until then Mam had had a trouble free pregnancy, therefore like so many other women at that time she had chosen to have her baby delivered at home. However on the night that I was born things didn't go quite as smoothly as she and Dad had expected. It seems that the midwife on duty was busy nursing another lady who lived just around the corner, and as the night wore on, Dad found himself racing frantically between the two houses, pleading with the nurse to do something – anything, that would help my Mam who was, by this time, in obvious distress.

Eventually I made my entry into the world. I was a blue baby, with the fateful umbilical cord tangled silently around my neck.

The other baby born that night was Alfred. Alfie, as I affectionately call him, played along side me during our early childhood. We shared birthday parties and birthday cakes. I remember how Dad used to light the coloured birthday candles for me to blow out and then light them once again for Alfie.

My baby days were apparently nothing out of the ordinary. It was only when I began to sit up did Mam and Dad notice my lack of balance. I had always had to be propped up and surrounded with lots of pillows and cushions. And it was the same when I began to toddle. I couldn't walk for more than a few steps without taking a tumble, usually onto the back of my head.

Whenever the family doctor was consulted he would simply say that I was a slow developer, but at the age of three, a specialist confirmed my parents fears. My brain had been damaged before or during my birth.

He sent Mam and Dad on their way with very little information or encouragement, but he did give them just one small piece of advice – I was to have plenty of fresh air and exercise.

When the seriousness of the situation was finally realised, Mam knew that there was only one of two paths that she could take. She could spend the rest of her life feeling bitter and resentful or she could stay close to the Lord and continue to seek His comfort within the warm, supporting community of the local Methodist church. Thankfully she chose the latter. And as for the people who knew me, well I was just 'Lynda.' A child who fell at the slightest touch, someone whose movements were awkward and jerky, someone whose speech was slurred and sometimes rather difficult to understand. I was just a little girl like all the rest, who loved and needed her Mam and Dad very much.

Yes, I can say in all honesty that if the Lord had to choose one baby that autumn night to be born just that little bit different to all the rest, then I really don't mind that He chose me… And who knows, had I been born without a disability, I may not be sitting here today, talking to you my dear friend.

Come, kneel beside me and join me in prayer...

Dear Lord,

Every day, in villages, towns and cities all across the world, disabled babies are being born into ordinary families. Their arrival will bring confusion, disappointment and possibly anger into the lives of the people around them.

To the parents and families of these children, we ask Lord for Your undivided attention. They will need a shoulder to weep on, an ear to whisper into, and a gentle hand to guide them into each new day. Stay close beside them Lord, and through Your Grace, the strength and energy which they will undoubtedly need, will flow freely from Your heart into theirs. Amen.

Baby days

THE RIGHT ROAD

It never ceases to amaze me the way in which I can spend hours and hours in another persons home and be completely unaware of my surroundings, yet within minutes of setting foot inside of my own front door, I've managed to notice every little detail. And it's always the same, it's always when I'm feeling totally relaxed, lying in some steamy bath or enjoying an early morning cup of tea, that I spy the offending rim of dust around the lamp shade or the curtain that has somehow lost its hook.

But for me, the discovery of a cobweb blowing cheekily in some corner has to be the most irritating and tantalising sight of all and I know that once a cobweb has been spotted that there'll be no peace in my mind until I've knocked it down.

At first I try flicking it with my duster and if this doesn't work I toss my yellow cloth high into the air once or twice. Usually this does the trick and the cobweb then comes floating down through the air, covering me in a veil of dirty grey lace. However, should the cobweb refuse to budge, I then need to go in search of something reliable to stand on… My small wooden chair.

It was my Nana who gave me the Sunday school chair. Sheer sentimentality prompted her to buy it when the property steward of the church announced that he had several for sale. At first we didn't quite know what to do with it. We had no earthly use for it in the house, but I knew that Nana would expect to see it whenever she happened to visit, and apart from that I hadn't the heart to banish it into the garage. Eventually we sanded it down, gave it a lick of paint and it's been with us ever since.

It is a very solid piece of furniture, considering it's more than a hundred years old – I don't think that fire or flood could even destroy it – and like some faithful servant, it has this uncanny knack of appearing first in one room and then in another, as if it's just aching to be of service again. It's certainly been well used, yet the funny thing is, it doesn't appear to have an air of neglect about it, quite the reverse in fact – it's a proud little chair.

Sometimes I look at it and wonder just how many little bottoms have smoothed its seat? Little bottoms belonging to tiny children with fertile minds. Minds which were ready for that important seed – the seed of faith.

At last we're on our way and although we may not have chosen the easiest or the shortest route to travel, at least we have the satisfaction of knowing that we are starting out on the right road. We can put away our maps and our compasses for an hour or two because the signpost in front of us points clearly the way ahead.

Don't you agree that the most valuable gift any adult can give to a child, is the gift of faith? And it's so easy, isn't it? All we need to do is to take them gently by the hand and lead them into a Sunday School. That was where my Mam took me at the age of three. I was one of the lucky ones!

Week after week, either she or Dad would help me to manoeuvre the curved wooden staircase, and clutching my 'star card' proudly in my hand, I would take my place in a room filled with thirty or so boisterous children.

Aunt Molly, the Sunday School teacher, had her own particular way of quietening us, and before too long we would all be seated on small wooden chairs, waiting to hear one of her familiar stories. Tales of fishing boats and loaves of bread… These tender stories, depending on the season, would be told to us Sunday after Sunday, and the funny thing was, they never lost any of their excitement in the re-telling.

It was in this familiar setting that I learnt about Jesus. I learnt about Him in stories and sung about Him in songs, until His name held no mystery for me. He became a living, breathing reality in my life. Someone who could always be depended upon be my friend.

It was in Sunday School where my own seed of faith was planted and with every story that I heard the seed went deeper. The sweet, childish hymns watered the seed, Aunty Molly's words strengthened the seed, and my heart has nurtured the seed ever since, willing it and willing it to grow.

Many of the children, who shared with me, those precious hours in Sunday School, worship beside me still. It seems that the seed was sown for them too, whilst they were seated on small wooden chairs, up a flight of worn wooden steps, in an upstairs room.

Dear Lord,

Thank you for the generations of Christian people who have travelled this road before us. It is due to their example and guidance that we have chosen to follow You. Help us to be like them in shouting the Good News across the busy streets and the prickly hedgerows, because after all Lord, it seems so selfish to keep such treasures to ourselves.

Bless the people who sow Your seed - the Sunday School teachers - who with Your help, can continue to lead our children out of the shadows and into the sunshine of the right road. Amen.

THE TOWN SQUARE

Fancy me having to come back to bed during the day – but that's what I've had to do again this morning. I got up as usual, pottered around the house, opening curtains and such like, and then because I was feeling so poorly, I decided to pamper myself with a couple of extra hours beneath the duvet.

It seems so strange lying here with nothing to do and already I'm beginning to feel quite guilty about it. There's a pile of ironing waiting to be finished and plenty of housework that should be done, but there's nothing that can't wait until I'm feeling a little better. All I have is a touch of flu....

Everything I need is here beside me. There's a hot water bottle to warm my feet on, a jug of orange juice to quench my thirst, and a jar of vaseline to smear beneath my bright red nose, and oh, yes, six huge white cotton hankies.

I even have the voice of my favourite Irish man coming across loud and clear on the bedroom radio, so I ask you, what more could a girl ask for? Well actually there is just one thing missing, or should I say one person missing, and that's 'Our Polly.' If only she could be here …

Shall we lay our knapsacks down for a little while and rest our weary legs here in the town square? I'll blow my runny nose and

17

wipe my streaming eyes, and then I'll be ready to tell you about 'Our Polly'.

Our Polly was my great, great aunt, consequently when I was born she was already approaching seventy. Even as a child it seems that Polly had had a poor constitution, suffering partial eyesight and severe deafness, but shortly after her marriage her health deteriorated still further and she became very ill with kidney failure and some form of facial paralysis. From then on Polly became a semi-invalid, virtually a recluse, visiting only her sister who lived just a few doors away from her.

Sadly, Polly remained childless, and it was only after she had endured many lonely years of widowhood that I appeared on the scene and seemingly gave her life a whole new meaning.

On sunny days she began pushing me in my pram, up and down the street and taking me for short walks into the town square, and incredulous as it may seem, she eventually found the confidence to make her way round to our house to spend a little time with me.

Whenever I was poorly as a child, Polly was the person I called out for and at the first sign of me having a temperature, Dad would light the fire in my bedroom and Polly would be brought to my bedside to keep me company (while Mam got on with her chores.) Mind you I've heard it said that Polly was more a nuisance than I was. She was forever calling down the stairs for one thing or another.

But can you imagine how wonderful it was for me to have a playmate who never seemed to be afraid of catching measles or chicken pox? Someone who could be persuaded to play any game that I suggested? Our days were happily spent doing jigsaw puzzles and leafing through picture books, and I can still remember that lovely 'soapy' smell that Polly had whenever we snuggled up close to share a cosy meal on a tray.

It's a strange coincidence that two of the most important people in my life have been profoundly deaf, making conversation with them for me almost impossible, yet the silent friendship which Polly and I shared was made up of lop-sided smiles and secret messages, and I'm sure that it was because we each recognised the frailty in one another that our relationship became extra special.

It's funny isn't it, the way that certain things stay in our memory? I can still remember how Polly used a piece of soft white lint to wipe my runny nose with – and shall I tell you a secret – on the nights when my heart pounds and my nerves jangle, the child in me still cries out for Polly. It's on nights such as these that my twitching fingers search for the piece of white lint which I keep beneath my pillow and the very feel of it's softness has the power to calm me and I sleep on.

What do you suppose a 'Guardian Angel' looks like? Well, Polly was small and slight, and always enveloped in a huge cotton apron that seemed to wrap round and around her meek and modest frame. And winter and summer alike, she would wear the same plain, dark clothes and black boots – the sort of boots that had all those tiny black buttons running up the front. Her short white hair was combed to one side, little girl fashion, and kept neatly in place by a huge black hairpin. But most important of all, Polly was gentle and kind and I loved her dearly.

Another thing I remember about Polly is how every Christmas morning I would present her with a box of her favourite sweeties, and even now when I'm busy doing my Christmas shopping, I can't help but finger the cellophane wrappings of the chocolate gingers, and I smile when I think of my darling Polly. Why did it never occur to me to buy her something really pretty, such as a soft colourful scarf perhaps, or a delicate brooch… Why do we always leave these things too late?

Now, the only tangible proof I have of Polly's existence is the white porcelain vase that takes pride of place on my mantle-piece, and inside one or two of my books, I find that she has written the initial 'P' to say that she has read them. But apart from 'Polly's Vase,' and a couple of dog-eared photographs, there's nothing to prove that Polly ever really existed. Yet have you noticed how angels such as Polly rarely do leave anything visible or valuable behind them – perhaps they're not meant to? Perhaps it's the aura that they leave behind which is far more lasting. Polly left me with the warmth of a million caring smiles, the sensation of a hundred secret hugs, and enough happy memories to last me a lifetime.

Dear Lord,

Bless the people who have the remarkable gift of bringing comfort into other people's lives, through their actions, their words, or merely their presence. Of all Your gifts Lord, this must surely be the greatest. Help us to cultivate our own special brand of comforting and to practise it at every opportunity. Amen.

All dressed up

THE COBBLED ALLEYWAY

I don't know about you, but whenever I visit a fairground, I love to watch the faces of the young folk as they leave a particularly dangerous or daring ride. They always look so invigorated and flushed with excitement that I can't help but wonder what it must feel like to travel at such great speed – my head goes dizzy if I look quickly from left to right.

How I admire the people who have fluidity of movement – people such as the skier and the wind-surfer and the chap on the motor bike, but I think most of all, I admire the audacity of the horse rider.

It's one of the few regrets I have, that I'll never be able to ride a horse. Of course there's nothing to stop me from sitting on one. I'm sure that someone would be kind enough to give me a 'leg up', but knowing my luck I'd probably finish up sitting the wrong way round and find a tail swishing in front of my nose. And you may think that this sounds ungrateful, but I don't like the idea of having to be set in position, of having my feet secured in the stirrups and the reigns placed in my hands. I would much rather give a little hitch and throw my leg across the horse's back (the way that Doris Day does in 'Calamity Jane'.)

I dare say that I'd be able to keep my balance long enough for someone to lead me round a stable yard or down a bridal path but you see this wouldn't really satisfy me. No, I wouldn't want to trot or canter – what I would really love to do would be to gallop…

I'd like to exert myself so much that my heart would pound loudly in my chest as I lay forward, close to the horse's mane. I'd love to feel the sheer power of the beast beneath me and know intuitively that I was in total control.

I can only imagine how wonderful it must be to thunder along some deserted windy beach on a glittering winter's morning, with gulls screaming overhead and breakers crashing and exploding inside my ears. We would chase the clouds together, the horse and I, and we would win…

Already the alleyway in front of us is beginning to incline just a little, so would you be kind enough to match your steps with mine. I'm sorry if I seem to be holding you back but I get out of puff so very quickly these days. Never mind, it's not as if we're in any hurry is it? We've still got plenty of time…

When I was a little girl, there were very few physical games that I could play outside. I could skip a little I remember, but usually I sat on the doorstep hugging my knees, quite content in watching my playmates romping around me, having fun. Their antics gave me many happy hours of enjoyment and the laughter that we all shared became an essential part of my everyday life.

At the age of four I was given a bright red tricycle as a Christmas present and as you can imagine, I was thrilled to pieces. This meant that at last I could really be part of the gang.

When I first began riding my trike, Dad would walk close by my side in case I should fall and together he and I must have travelled hundreds of miles, roaming up and down the rows of long terraced side streets. Every now and again I remember how he used to take me to where there was a small incline and believe me, to me it seemed like a mountain. It demanded all of my energy just to keep the wheels of the trike turning.

"Give me a push Dad," I used to plead with him but of course he wouldn't. Laughing he would say, "Go on, you can do it," and not wanting to disappoint him I would huff and puff until I'd reached the top of the hill, rosy-cheeked and triumphant.

This was typical of the way in which Dad made exercise seem like fun for me and eventually his patience and my perseverance paid off and the flabby weak muscles in my legs grew stronger and stronger, and so did my confidence. As you know, northern men are renowned for their strength of character and Dad was no exception. I remember his favourite saying during those early years – "If at first you don't succeed, try and try again." How I grew tired of hearing those words. Yet the independent spirit that Dad nurtured in me as a child has certainly stood me in good stead for the times that lay ahead and occasionally I wonder just how I'm going to manage now that he isn't here beside me, spurring me on.

Getting back to my trike… Now behind our house we had a back alley and likewise on the other side of the street and these two cobbled back arches formed a sort of race track, as me and my pals pedalled furiously first up one bumpy back alley, across the street, and then down the other. Round and round we would all race, bobbing our heads low beneath the lines of billowing white washing. My friends passed me by so often that it was hard to tell whether I was beginning one lap or ending another, but it didn't matter, I was very happy. Come to think of it, those rides on my trike are the nearest feelings of exhilaration that I have ever known. Not that I ever felt the wind whipping through my hair or anything like that, but I remember it felt good.

Physical exhilaration, I doubt I'll ever know, but exhilaration of the heart, ah…well, that's another matter.

Dear Lord,

Thank You for the people whose words of encouragement have spurred us on when we've grown weary or dispirited. Help us to realise that they have had our best interests at heart. All we have ever yearned for in the way of prizes Lord, are their smiles of approval and of course, whenever possible, a smile from Your lips too. Amen.

Riding my trike

THE BUSY THOROUGHFARE

It's funny isn't it, how when we're on holiday we inevitably find a café or a bar which suits us down to a 'T.' A place which oozes atmosphere – a place where we feel at ease. Usually we stumble upon these places at the very beginning of our holiday and time and time again our wanderings take us back to the place where we have been made to feel most welcome.

This year, strolling through the resort we found a bar called Sinatra's. Well actually that's not strictly true, I have a sneaking feeling that Sinatra's bar found us! There we were, just sauntering along, minding our own business when we heard the voice of Ole Blue Eyes being ingeniously amplified into the warm evening air. And just like the peel of church bells, it was charming a steady flow of holiday makers into its web of enchantment.

On our last evening I put on my 'best frock.' (You know the one I mean. The dress that we ladies keep to wear at the end of our holiday, hoping that it's going to show off our suntans.) And without any conferring we knew instinctively where our feet would be taking us.

It's laughable but had I been at home I would have been curled up on the sofa with my usual Horlicks and biscuits, but because I was winding my way back to Sinatra's bar, all thoughts of sleep were far, far away. I was ready to 'Boogie the night away. (Why is it that we feel so much more alive when we're on holiday – Could it be something that they put in the water?)

Anyway, getting back to Sinatra's bar…We'd just got settled into our seats when a young woman and her elderly father walked into the bar. She had Downs Syndrome. They came and sat beside us and as the night wore on I couldn't help but notice that her feet were tapping like mine to the music, so it seemed the most natural thing in the world for me to invite her to dance.

We danced and danced – she didn't seem to want to stop – and needless to say, there wasn't any fancy footwork or any outstanding movements on our part, we simply swayed and rocked to the music. But at least we were involved, taking part. Eventually my feet and legs screamed out for mercy, so in smiling agreement we wove our way back across the dance floor and flopped like rag-dolls into our seats.

Shyly, her Dad thanked me for dancing with her – the pleasure had been all mine …I knew from experience just how much it hurt to be left on the outside, and I knew also that the pain of exclusion was a terrible and excruciating pain to bear.

Before getting caught up in this busy thoroughfare, shall we sit for a few moments on the low, stone wall of this playground? As the children behind us chant their nursery rhymes and turn their skipping ropes, I'll begin to tell you about my early days at school.

In the beginning my parents were my champions and even today, to a certain degree, they still are. Like all good parents they have always done what they thought was best for me so when the time came for me to start full time education they saw it as my right to be placed in a school with able bodied children.

In those days there was no need to enrol with any particular school, it was an automatic procedure that when your baby's birth was registered, a place was made available for them at their nearest infant school. Still you can imagine can't you, the relief on Mam's face when she led me into the classroom on that very first morning and saw my name chalked up on the blackboard.

Knowing Mam as I do, I suspect that leaving me behind in the care of some stranger must have been an enormous wrench for her, and I can only begin to appreciate how she must have worried and fretted for the rest of that day, visualising the fearful things which were happening to me, when in reality I was having a wonderful time. It was only when I was in the playground that I felt really frightened and nervous. Everyone around me seemed to move so quickly that I was always afraid of being knocked down.

Being an only child I was eager to make friends and before too long I found myself surrounded by a small group of children, who over the years became fiercely protective towards me. If ever cruel remarks were hurled my way, it was these same little companions who cushioned the blows and who coaxed me back into a bright circle of friendship. I soon came to realise just how much I depended on these new found friends for the practical help which they could give me, and together we learnt from one another those first vital lessons of human kindness.

After P.E. lessons I would turn around and tiny fingers, fingers that weren't as clumsy as mine, would be there to button up my dress for me or to fasten my shoe laces. And in art classes it was the same. I only had to ask for help and someone would be at my side to cut out intricate shapes or to stick gluey pieces of paper together. Come to think of it, I must have been quite a nuisance in those days – yet saying that, I managed to draw the attention of quite a few boyfriends! Maybe because I always seemed to be the proverbial damsel in distress!

Classes were large I remember, and if I was an extra burden for my teachers, I can only send them my apologies, but quite honestly they never showed me any impatience. If anything they warmed towards me and helped me in every way that they could. Perhaps to them I was viewed as some form of challenge, I really can't say, I only know that I loved being at school and even today whenever I walk into a classroom the smell of chalk stirs in me an excitement that is hard to define.

Although my writing was poor, I found that I had a healthy appetite for knowledge and that I was quick to learn, but as you can imagine, gym lessons were always a nightmare. It didn't take me long to realise my inadequacies when it came to gamesmanship. Let's face it, what child in their right mind would genuinely want me in their team? What chance had they of scoring any team points with me dropping beanbags every two seconds? I remember being pushed and shoved from one team to another until eventually one or another of my friends felt sorry for me and cajoled the rest of her team into letting me join them. More often than not I would have to fight back the tears until I reached home and only then would I allow them to flow. As always Mam and Dad did their best to make light of my problems but naturally my pain was their pain, and the bruising went deep. However, laughter always predominated in our house and my tears would soon be forgotten, and the next morning you would find me back in the school-yard, smiling shyly at the children who had hurt me, but somehow never quite forgiving them for the humiliation which they had caused.

When I was seven I remember volunteering to conduct the school choir through the hymn, "Jesus good above all other." Whether it was the tune, the words, or the occasion I don't really know, I only know that something compelled me to struggle up onto the makeshift platform baton in hand, to take part in that memorable performance.

Even in those early days it seems as if music was able to weave its magical spell around me, melting away any self doubts which I may have had and giving me that invaluable inner strength.

Dear Lord,
Help us to teach our children the true meaning of acceptance. By our example, let us show them how easy it is to draw into our own circle of friends, perhaps one companion who is that little bit 'different'. Open our children's eyes to the child in the corner Lord, and encourage them to reach out their hands so that everyone in the classroom is included in the fun. Amen.

With my infant school friends

THE RESTRICTED AREA

I'm sure that most of us go through life with one sort of hangup or another and that given the chance we could all find something about our faces or our figures that we would dearly love to change. Yet saying that, I've found that life has a curious way of smoothing out our imperfections – it has this wonderful knack of making us feel comfortable in our own individual skins. The secret of it all is to think kindly about ourselves and try to be content with how we look and who we are.

I remember how back in my youth, I seemed to be forever scowling at my face in the mirror. Yet here I am on the verge of middle age, giving that same funny face a friendly wink. And I'm glad to say that the eyes that laugh back into mine have more than just a hint of mischief about them. And where once upon a time, the glimpse of my reflection in some shop window would have had the power to alarm me, I find that these days, should I happen to meet myself in the street, I have to stop my legs from giving a hop, skip and a jump.

But joking apart, overriding all of my physical peculiarities, the greatest stumbling block of all has been my poor speech. My voice implies to the world that my words are just not worth listening to.

This inability to speak clearly is something that I've always taken seriously. Society has never allowed me to disregard it or treat it lightly and if you were to ask me today, which facet of my disability has caused me the most hurt and frustration, then I would tell you quite honestly that it has been my speech.

A long time ago, when I first began writing for pleasure, I remember giving a friend of mine a couple of my articles to read, and a few weeks later, when she handed them back to me she said, "I enjoyed your stories Lynda, but you don't write the way you speak." Her comments went straight to the very heart of me, yet I knew that what she had just said was true. I don't write the way I speak...

It's as if when I'm in conversation with someone, I never quite manage to get my tongue around the words that I would really like to use. I tend to use words that are easy for me to pronounce instead. Consequently, to everyone but myself, my writing and my voice will always stay worlds apart.

I think that's the thing I've missed more than anything else in my life – two way conversations – getting to know other people and them getting to know me.

My granddad died some years ago now, just ten days before his hundredth birthday and for as long as I can remember he had been profoundly deaf, consequently, he and I were never able to indulge in an adult conversation. Obviously, he spoke to me, but I hadn't the strength to project my voice so that he could hear my answers. I had so many questions to ask this man that I loved. So many things to tell him... But never mind, maybe one day in heaven we can talk over our lifetime experiences. It's a comforting thought...

But it's when I'm in chapel that my voice disappoints me the most. I, who have so much to thank Him for, can only stand and whisper my songs of praise when in all honesty I would much rather be raising the rafters.

Forgive my tears of frustration, I'll soon wipe them away, and then together you and I can look beyond these steel barricades and into the restricted area. Into the place where only clear voices are listened to and respected...

If I could have just one wish granted, it would be for a clear voice. A voice that commands attention. There's so much that I want to say. Words tumble lazily from my lips, making hardly any sense at all, yet my views and opinions are very much alive, locked deep within me, panting and gasping to be heard and understood.

It's funny but when I speak, my mind tricks me into believing that my speech is perfect, but I have only to look into the face of the listener to know that this isn't so.

Yet when I was five years old I was given the opportunity to improve my speech and every Friday morning I would be taken along to the speech therapy clinic that my head teacher had suggested I attend.

Children's minds are strange places aren't they? And I would love to be able to analyse my thoughts for you as I sat opposite the young woman who was qualified to help me. But at that point in time I honestly didn't realise that I had a problem. I wasn't aware that for the rest of my life I was going to be judged and categorised with every word that I uttered.

Even at that early age though, I must have had a sense of pride, because I can still remember how degrading it felt to be asked to make patterns with the coloured building blocks that were stacked on the table in front of me. I really couldn't understand the connection. Here I was, supposedly being taught how to speak correctly and I was being asked to play games... And baby games at that! It was all so very confusing.

If only the therapist had taken the time to talk to me. If only she'd explained a little about what she was hoping to achieve and what she was expecting from me. But no one attempted an explanation and I felt like an idiot. Yes even at five years old I wanted some answers, some information, but the questions I wanted to ask were stuck in my throat. It was a vicious circle.

What would I do I wonder, if I were given the chance to go back into that room again today? Would I try harder to achieve some small degree of improvement? We'll never know will we? That day has long since passed and rarely do we get the opportunity to explore the same avenue.

So I've decided that my pen shall be my voice now. All my thoughts, emotions and passions can serge through the veins of my left hand so that it can fly across the page, never ceasing. I pray that my writing will embrace the lonely and encourage the weak, but most of all I want my words to dance for joy and give testimony to my faith.

Dear Lord,

Give an extra ounce of courage to the people who live their lives with any sort of speech impediment. You must surely know how difficult it is for us to find our rightful place in this world.

Help strangers, hearing our voices for the first time, to be slow in their judgement of us and bless them with a little of Your patience and understanding during the first few moments of our two way conversations.

All it takes Lord is for them to have ears that really listen and a heart that genuinely cares. Amen.

THE BUSTLING MARKET PLACE

Unfortunately there are two factors in my life that I will never be able to change, no matter how hard I might try. One of these is my disability and the other is the fact that I am an only child. And strange as it may seem, I find that the older I become the importance of my disability fades and my longing for a brother or sister increases.

I do try to understand the quandary that Mam and Dad must have faced when they discussed the possibility of having another child. They were genuinely afraid that by giving me a sibling they would have pushed me out of the picture and into a shadowy corner – into a place where I was sure to have become shy and self-conscious.

Of course I can see the logic in this train of thought and yes, perhaps they were right, perhaps having another youngster in the family would have shown me just how disabled I really was, but I myself would have been willing to have taken this chance.

Common sense tells me that I wouldn't have been able to do everything that my sibling could do, nor could I have taken part in many of their activities, and yes maybe there would have been times when I would have held them back or caused them embarrassment, but in my mind these are mere trivialities. What I am sure about is that the love and laughter which had circulated so freely in our house, could have easily been stretched four ways, and with Mam and Dad to guide us, I'm sure my sibling and I would have grown up together, bonded firmly with love.

I can't help but imagine, just how wonderful it would have been to have had a brother or sister to walk life's journey with me. Someone who knew me well - someone who I knew well - someone who would have been there for me whenever I needed help in carrying my load. Someone I could have put my arm around and together we would have laughed at the world and said, "Look at the pair of us. Aren't we lucky to have each other!"

I'd like to believe that my brother or sister would have needed me just as much as I needed them and that ours wouldn't have been a one-sided relationship. I can think of hundreds of ways in which I could have proved my love for them… I would have enjoyed being an aunt for instance – the baby-sitting, the holidays together…

I can't help but sigh when I think of all those hugs that I've missed and of the quiet conversations that would have passed so easily between us. I don't know about you, but sometimes I used to find it difficult - discussing personal problems with my parents - even parents who were as loving and as caring as mine - I didn't like worrying them unnecessarily. Therefore to have another person's ear to confide in, would have been very comforting indeed.

Have I told you how lovely it is - having your company on this journey of ours? Would you mind if I put my arm through yours as we walk through this bustling market place together?

Loneliness was something I never experienced as a child, I seem to recall only the sunshine of friendships, and looking back, I can see now that it was my childhood experiences which shaped the contours of my personality, and without doubt, it was my family and friends who helped to mould this happy heart.

Whether I was on the doorstep, in the playground, or by the fireside, other youngsters played beside me, and I can truthfully say that I never gave a thought to being an only child – never questioned the fact. I saw my friends with their brothers and sisters and I felt no jealousy at all.

Shortly after I started junior school, we moved house, and just five doors away from our new home lived my Aunt and Uncle, and my two young cousins. Naturally, they became a happy extension to our own small family and I often reminisce about the fun and close association that we all shared.

Also my friend Anne lived just around the corner to our new house, which meant that we were able to call on one another without having too many busy roads to cross.

Come to think of it, throughout my life there have been very few places, apart from my own home, where I've felt totally and completely at ease, but Anne's house was definitely one of them. Being there was like being in a tiny pocket of security, and the acceptance which I craved in society, was found right there in the very heart of Anne's family.

It was in Anne's front room where I began my life-long interest in lawn tennis. Not playing it of course, just watching it. For hours on end, Anne and I would sit together on the sofa, our eyes glued to the small black and white television screen in the corner of the room, and Anne's Dad, in his softly spoken voice, would confidently explain to us the rudiments of the game. He taught us about volleys and aces, about lobs and deuces, but most important of all, he showed us how good it felt to cheer another person on. Every time a point was scored at Wimbledon, shouts and cheers would go up all around the room, and by the time a game, set and match had been fought over and won, the atmosphere in the whole house had become almost electric.

36

I remember never wanting to leave Anne's house – I felt so much at home there. So much so, that when the time came for Anne's Mum to lay the table for tea, I used to hold my breath, praying fervently that there would be a place setting for me – and there always was.

I had another special friend around this time – a scruffy mongrel called Jock. Animals are such wonderful companions aren't they, so relaxing and comforting to be with, and I can still remember the smell and texture of Jock's thick, black and white curly coat, and how as a child I used to put my cheek close to his and whisper all my secrets into his sympathetic ear. He used to put his head to one side, just as if he was considering my problems, and his big dark brown eyes would laugh and cry simultaneously with mine.

He was a bit of a rogue was my pal Jock. A bit of a loner. He was forever wandering around the town and getting into scrapes. And should any of the family happen to spot him trotting round the market place, they would do their utmost to avoid him because he always seemed to be in mischief of one sort or another. For instance Mam often spied him coming out of the Catholic Church and leaving his calling card on the side of the big double doors. Had he been to confession we used to wonder? Well knowing Jock, he probably had!

Jock was with us for fourteen years and I know my Mam won't mind me telling you this, but she still has his leash hanging from a hook in her kitchen. A constant reminder of a trusty friend.

So this loneliness which keeps creeping up on me, where on earth do you suppose it is coming from? Is it yet another symptom of middle age? I don't know - I haven't got a clue – I only know that in my mind there isn't a lovelier sound in the entire world than brothers and sisters talking and laughing together. So will you do me a huge favour? Next time you see your brother or sister, will you give them a big hug and pretend that it's from me?

37

Dear Lord,

Bless the people, who for whatever reason, find themselves walking down a lonely road. Keep their hearts buoyant by allowing Your presence to be felt at every corner and crossroad.

Help us to be aware of the lonely people around us and give us courage to reach out to them all with a smile and a hug. Take us to the places where we are most needed Lord. To the solitary bed-sit, to the high rise flat or perhaps into a teeming home where a young mother feels captive.

Keep on reminding us that loneliness comes cloaked in many disguises and grant us a little of Your perception so that we can recognise it behind the false laughter and the unshed tears. Amen.

With my best friend Anne

THE BLIND ALLEY

Believe it or not, it takes me the best part of a day to do my ironing, yet funnily enough, it's the one chore that I thoroughly enjoy. It demands so little of my energy and no one invades my privacy as I stand in the corner of my living room, my music centre by my side.

You could say that music is my passion – it sets my spirit free – and on ironing day, melodies perfume the air like the scent of summer roses, and I breathe deeply.

It only takes a familiar tune and whoosh... My ironing board becomes a jet plane, taking me to holiday destinations where laughter comes easy and lovemaking is often. I feel sunshine on my face and soft warm sand beneath my feet as I sip glasses of wine in Portugal and cups of cappuccino in Rome.

Music somehow liberates my wooden muscles because it's only at my ironing board that I can waltz my way through Vienna and Cha Cha across South America with a grace that is foreign to me. The faster the rhythm, the faster I iron.

I tap dance my way down 42nd Street, jive with John Travolta and pas de deux with the best of them. Me, whose legs will never be cajoled into dancing and whose arthritic fingers will never be able to play a sonata, would give almost anything to be able to express my self with music, but at least at my ironing board I find great joy in just listening.

Vivaldi leads me down leafy lanes and with Grieg I climb into mountains, feeling refreshed and rejuvenated by the clear bracing air.

Sinatra's voice caresses the place that no other voice can reach and there's something about Pavarotti's voice that touches my very soul.

And just like a boisterous wind that whips up the scurrying leaves, the music of Verdi can stir my thoughts to such an extent that my ironing board becomes my soap-box – I put the world to rights there – and no one is beside me to shout me down.

Tchaikovsky's music has the power to rouse forgotten feelings deep within me, and it's whilst I'm at my ironing board that I dream my dreams. Dreams for tomorrow, next week, next year… I plan my future there and no one can sneer at me.

But if I spoke the truth, the music that I love listening to most, is the music that tiptoes across my brow and turns my ironing board into my alter. My own special place… The place where I whisper my prayers and count my blessings. It's there that I have the time to remember other people and I pray silently and sincerely for their needs. It's also the place where I talk to you, my dear friend.

So now you know my secret! Without music in my life I would undoubtedly whither and without my ironing board I'm sure that my creativity would cease.

To keep our spirits high, why don't you and I try our hand at making some music? The blind alley in front of us is a dark and dreary place, but doesn't despair; we won't even begin to notice it. We'll be far too busy banging our drums and crashing our cymbals. So move over James Last and make way for us.

From as far back as I can remember, music has always been able to do wonderful things to my heart, and I must have been around the age of seven or eight when I first began to pester my Mam and Dad into letting me have a few piano lessons.

I remember that I had just been on a theatre trip with my classmates to see the ballet, Swan Lake and I'd been absolutely thrilled by it. So much so, when my birthday came around, I was given the full orchestral score on a long-playing record. Come to think of it, I've still got that self same record in my record collection today and very scratched it is too. Anyway, getting back to my piano lessons...

Whether I imagined myself to be the next Tchaikovsky, I really can't say, I just know that I loved the idea of making a melody appear out of clear air, and because Mam and Dad envisaged piano lessons as being the perfect excerise for my stiff fingers and hands, they finally gave in to my continual requests. I think that's the thing that I've loved most about my Mam and Dad – the thing that I'm most grateful to them for – they've never stopped me or tried to dissuade me from having a go at things, even though they have known what the consequences were likely to be.

Eventually, an old creaking piano was carried into our front parlour and very soon afterwards, a lady was found who was willing to teach me.

Miss Callender was a very genteel lady, who was blessed with what can only be described as supernatural patience. Week after week she taught me until I could play fairly simple pieces of music with ease, and play them quite adeptly with my left hand. But alas, when the time came for my right hand to be introduced to the piano keys, it rebelled like some naughty child, and refused to co-operate.

How well I remember struggling to coax my fingers into action – I did so much want to play – but it was no use, after just a few months I began to realise that my hands were never going to play the piano in the way that I had intended, and the day finally dawned when I had to concede defeat.

Looking back, I can see now, that this was my first real taste of disappointment and between you and me, it left a taste on my tongue as bitter and as sour as crab apples.

In the end I had no alternative but to say goodbye to Miss Callender and to thank her for doing her very best to help me and I often wonder whether her heart had ached as much as mine had done, the evening we said our goodbyes in her front parlour?

As I write this chapter, I can actually hear someone playing the piano in the living room downstairs. Their fingers are running skilfully up and down the keys as they practise their scales. Can you guess who it could be?

Dear Lord,

Thank You for the music makers. For the people who manipulate our hearts to such an extent that they rise up, above the pain and anxiety of our earthly bodies, to a place where you alone Lord have access.

Bless the composer, the choirmaster and the street busker and help us all to cultivate whenever and where ever we can, any hint of musical talent amongst our young people. Amen.

With my wonderful mam

THE ILLUMINATED HIGH STREET

In this life, all that I can ever hope to be is a spectator, and I really don't mind, just as long as I am allowed to have a window seat from which to view the world. Yet once a year, in November, I'm afforded more that this when I'm thrust into the very heart of things during the weekend that I spend in London.

Only there, amidst the impressive breathing buildings am I able to melt into the background and become almost invisible – just the way I like it. The people thronging around Oxford Street are far too preoccupied with their own Christmas shopping to cast any glances my way, so when I'm amongst them my imagination is given a free rein. No longer am I a housewife from Cleveland. In my mind I can be anyone that I choose to be….

I can be a flamboyant artist with an exhibition at one of the many art galleries. I can be a vivacious chorus girl on her way to rehearsals at a West End theatre…I can even be a perfumed sophisticate, with an invitation to a cocktail party at the glitzy and exclusive Savoy Hotel. Oh yes… I have a simply wonderful time playing games with my imagination.

I'm giving away secrets here, but I have a special bottle of cologne which I keep specifically for my weekend in London and the minute I arrive in the City I douse myself in it. One whiff of its perfume heightens my sensitivity. My heartbeat quickens, my pulses race and my eyes are opened wider than ever by the magnificent sights which I see.

I adore everything about London. The noises, the traffic, the crowds. I don't even mind being pushed and shoved a little. It proves to me that I'm really alive – participating in life – rubbing shoulders with other human beings. And you may think that this sounds crazy, but it's almost as if I have another persons energy coursing through my veins, because it's only when I'm walking in and around London that I feel really vibrant and carefree... Don't get me wrong – I still walk slowly and clumsily. I still trip over the odd kerbstone and the odd cracked pavement – but there's a vitality in my step which I've yet to experience back home.

At every coffee shop that I pass, these old bones cry out for comfort and my aching back implores me to rest, but I just laugh at my aches and pains and take a pill. I've no intention of missing even one second of my weekend because I know that the excitement that I'm tasting has to last me for at least another three hundred and sixty two more days in the year – or who knows - maybe even longer.

For one glorious weekend I'm able to window shop to my hearts content and do all of the things that visitors to the city are supposed to do. I explore the sights and sounds of Covent Garden, enthuse over a couple of West End shows, and usually by the Saturday morning you'll find me with blistering feet, tiptoeing my way around the elaborate displays of Christmas decorations on the fourth floor at Harrods.

This year, as I wandered childlike amongst the glittering arrays of garlands and festive trimmings, I found myself remembering some Christmas decorations of a very different kind...

Why don't you and I turn up our collars and sit for a while on the corner of this illuminated High street. We'll snuggle up cosily together and watch the Christmas shoppers as they go slithering and sliding past. Then, once I've taken my painkiller, I'll tell you about the Christmas preparations that I often took part in.

Every year, on precisely the third Monday in November, I would rush excitedly out of school and head straight for the chapel school-room, which was, by the time that I arrived, already buzzing with frenzied activity. The folk in there were busy getting ready for their annual 'At Homes.'

Overnight it seemed as if all the Nanas, Grannies, and Aunt's belonging the church, had momentarily tossed aside their knitting needles and their crocheting hooks and had assumed the roles of artistic designers – with great powers to transform – and we the children were more than happy to take part in the amazing transformation.

No instructions were necessary. We knew exactly what was required of us. So with our tongues peeping from the corner of our mouths and a watchful eye peering over our shoulders, we would get on with the job in hand.

On single strands of white cotton we threaded milk bottle tops and cotton wool balls and these we then attached to a stronger much longer length of thread that was hoisted high above our heads and secured safely in place. Line upon line of these garlands would be painstakingly fashioned until the whole of the ceiling had been completely obliterated by them and it was only then, when all the trimmings were in place that we allowed ourselves to sit back and admire our handy work. Every year, declaring our latest decorations to be prettier and more spectacular than ever before.

On the first night of the 'At Homes' as we the children squatted on the floor, close to the stage and the footlights, I remember how the excitement and noise in the room had simmered and simmered until it had threatened to bubble over. It was an evening for renewing

45

acquaintances and for delighting in the familiar warm hospitality of the church.

The decorations that wafted gently above our heads weren't the only changes which had taken place in the chapel schoolroom. Over to our right the vestry bulged with goodies and chocolate novelties. Where for just a few pennies, toffees could be bought. Toffees that could be popped into our mouths the minute that the performance began. And makeshift stalls had also miraculously appeared. Stalls which were draped and strewn with fancywork and needlecraft. We knew these to be simply magical places, where later in the evening we would be sure to find that perfect gift for our mothers Christmas stocking.

In the beehive of a kitchen, over to our left, rosy cheeked ladies with capable hands were busily preparing plate after plate of supper… A sandwich, a pastry, a cake… And hundreds of rattling cups and saucers would be lined up like soldiers, waiting for the end of the evening when the huge fat brown tea pot would deliver the scalding hot tea.

And it was just when I was beginning to feel all fidgety and impatient, and finding it impossible to keep still for a moment longer, that the light in the vestry would be extinguished and the door to the kitchen would be quietly closed. Then a person with a sincere voice would stand up and say how very pleased he was to be spending the evening amongst us. Then a prayer would be softly spoken in unison and a favourite old hymn would be gloriously sung. And then someone at the back of the hall – usually a man with a kind face, who knew his task well – would amazingly flick off the light switches at precisely the right moment.

It was then, in the semi-darkness that I would gaze up, heart pounding. Not at the stage or at the players. No my eyes travelled higher and higher until I had to tilt back my head. Gone were the milk bottle tops and the cotton wool balls and in their place floated a swirling mass of snowflakes and scattered wondrously amongst them, a thousand silver stars sparkled and shone.

And do you know what? Not even the garlands that I saw on display at Harrods this year could possibly compere to the memory of those starry decorations.

I wonder what today's youngsters would make of our primitive attempts to enhance the chapel schoolroom? I dare say that they wouldn't be greatly impressed. But to me and my small friends, and I'm sure to our Nanas, Grannies, and Aunts, those dazzling, swirling snowstorms had always heralded the true beginning of Christmas.

Dear Lord.

Thank You for our Christmas memories. For the sights, smells and sounds that come flooding back into our minds whenever we begin to decorate our homes for Christmas.

In the flames of our Christmas candles Lord, let us see the faces of the people who have been dear to us. In the carols that we sing let us hear once more their voices, and in the lights that twinkle around the tree, bring to our minds, their smiles.

Only then Lord, when our memories of past Christmases are gay and bright will the spirit and true beauty of the season truely surround us. Amen.

THE FIRST VANTAGE POINT

No doubt you'll find this hard to believe, I must admit I have difficulty in believing it myself, but last Monday I became a member of a Health Club.

The idea first began germinating in my mind about a fortnight ago when an introductory leaflet was stuffed through our letter box, and being the inquisitive person that I am, I read it from cover to cover and found the concept of 'working out' strangely appealing. However, the mental picture of me prancing around in some leotard and tights wasn't quite so attractive but after mulling it over in my mind for a couple of days – should I go or shouldn't I? – I finally decided to go ahead and make the necessary appointment. You should know me well enough by now to know that I'll try my hand at almost anything!

Naturally, because of my disability, I was a little apprehensive as to the sort of reception that I would receive and during the drive to the Health Club I did my best to prepare myself for the possibility of being denied membership. To be honest with you, I wasn't looking forward to another kick in the teeth but surprise, surprise, I was made to feel most welcome.

After being introduced to one of the instructors, I was given the usual royal tour of the building and you know how it is when you feel as if you should be contributing something to the conversation? So I said daft things like, 'The sauna looks inviting,' and 'I can't wait to try out those toning tables,' when all the time, the room which was appealing to me the most was the coffee lounge. But of course I couldn't voice such a thing, so I bit my tongue, put on my most serious expression and tried at least to look as if I was interested in getting fit.

Up until Monday I had never been inside a gym before and as I walked with the instructor through the various rooms I couldn't help but notice how gruesome some of the apparatus looked. I'm not joking, but some of the equipment looked like huge terrifying monsters just waiting to pounce, and to make matters worse, everyone around me were 'Gladiator' look-a-likes. In fact there was one point in the evening when I found myself thinking, 'What in heavens name am I doing in a place like this,' and between me and you, I was tempted to make a run for it – but of course I didn't – I didn't want to lose face – consequently I stayed where I was and tried my best to concentrate on what the young instructor was saying.

Eventually the time came for me to change into my trainers and after bending down to fasten my shoe laces, I nearly confessed then and there that that had been enough exercise for me!

What a laugh it was doing the different tests. I was asked to pull on one bar and push on another – I was out of breath even before any weights had been added – and as I was led panting and gasping from one tortuous machine to the next I could feel the colour in my cheeks becoming redder and redder. Consequently, by the time I'd finished blowing into the various tubes that were being handed to me, you can imagine, my face was almost fluorescent.

During one test, I was encouraged to exert myself as much as possible so that my quickening heartbeat could be monitored, but try as I might there wasn't a bleep to be heard. Never mind the instructor, even I was beginning to be concerned. I was sure that I'd been breathing on arrival…

I was just beginning to relax and enjoy myself a little when the trainer produced a pair of pincers from her tunic pocket and began to measure the excess fat around my waistline – well I ask you, what was I to do? - Except breathe in!

Gradually I became aware that I was causing a certain amount of polite curiosity from the people around me, after all I wasn't the usual run of the mill member, and it was with my usual shyness that I acknowledged and returned the smiles which were coming my way. I may be wrong but it seemed to me as if my onlookers were giving me a silent ripple of approval for simply having a go.

Obviously every test that I did, I was below average, (apart from the excess fat, that is) but let's face it, it would have been silly of me to expect otherwise, wouldn't it? Yet saying that, I surprised myself with the amount of exercise that I managed to do and I came away from the health club purring with satisfaction and feeling like the cat that had got the cream.

What a delicious sleep I had that night. I drifted into oblivion with a smile on my lips and I remember thinking to myself just before I dropped off, "If ever I reach 'Gladiator' status, I'll call myself the 'Tiger.'

Whilst we're in a sporting mood, why don't you and I do a few press-ups, here by the gates of our local clinic. We'll flex our muscles and tone our biceps and then if I have any puff left I'll tell you about the times when I used to come along here as a child for my annual check-ups.

Periodically a crisp white card would menacingly appear on our bristly doormat and although it was never welcomed, it was a summons that we didn't dare to disregard.

For the next few weeks it would stand defiantly on our mantle-piece, propped up by the knick knacks and the ticking clock, a constant reminder of the disability that I was doing my best to ignore.

Every time my eyes came to rest on it, my physical condition would be dragged to the very forefront of my young mind once more, consequently, over the years, I came to detest the very sight of those starched appointment cards.

From the moment of the cards' arrival I could sense Mam's nervousness and try as I might I could never figure out why she should feel so apprehensive. After all, we both knew what would take place at the consultation, we even knew the words which would be spoken, yet for some unknown reason, whenever the forthcoming appointment was mentioned, Mam's smile would falter just a little and butterflies would start flapping and fluttering around my tummy as though they were demented.

It's funny but when I was young, red-letter days such as birthdays and Christmas's used to snake their way through the calendar, but the dreadful dates, such as the date of my check-up, used to bound along at a alarming pace and in no time at all I would find myself sitting beside my Mam in the stark, sombre waiting room of our local clinic.

Thinking back, Dad never came with us. I wonder why? It wasn't as if he didn't care about my progress! I can only presume that in those days the men folk went to work and the women in the family took care of everything else.

On entering the room, the same room that was being used for my speech therapy classes, Mam and I would be greeted as usual by Dr. Adamson, the orthopaedic paediatrician. And whether it was due to Dr. Adamson's cold professional attitude, or whether it was due to Mam's nervousness, I really can't say, I only know that there was a tension in that room that did little to ease my trepidation.

I remember how Mam's voice always took on a different tone whenever the doctor addressed her. She sounded a little bit too bright somehow, not at all like she did at home, and her smiles were always overshadowed by the anxiety which was mirrored in her eyes. Mam may have been able to fool Dr. Adamson but she certainly didn't fool me. I knew that she hated these interviews and yet I had no idea why.

When the preliminaries were over, the examination would then take on its usual form. First my legs would be measured and tested for their strength and then my upper body movement would be assessed. And I can still remember how difficult this proved to be for me and how I would push and push on the doctor's arms as hard as I possibly could, praying that there would be some small degree of improvement. And in the back of my mind I knew that I wasn't exerting myself for the benefit of Dr. Adamson. I knew that I was exerting myself purely for my Mam's sake. I desperately needed to see one of her warm familiar smiles again. The kind of smile which she kept especially for me. Unfortunately these particular smiles never seemed to materialise, I saw only the false fabricated smiles that she kept specifically for Dr. Adamson.

Apparently the muscles in my legs were strong – thanks to my trike – but the muscles in my arms and my upper body were always very poor. And looking back I can see now that the only good thing to come out of these consultations was the fact that I was able to tell the doctor quite truthfully, that I was experiencing no pain whatsoever.

When the examination was over and I was dressed once more in my new white vest and panties, I remember how the familiar questions would then begin to fly across the table, accompanied by the same dull explanations from Dr. Adamson. And over the years, as I sat listening in on these discussions, putting two and two together in my own little head, I came to the conclusion that this thing called spasticity was never going to go away. Whatever it was, it was going to stay with me forever. There wasn't going to be any miracle cure that would relieve me of its symptoms. No medicine on earth was going to straighten my limbs or cause my muscles to relax. No wonder drug was going to keep my head up straight or stop the saliva from dripping off my chin when it was least expected. In other words, there was nothing at all that the doctor could do about it.

Year after year Mam and I would arrive at the clinic, searching for some kind of magical solution, but alas, there were never any pleasant surprises. Yet the funny thing was, as we stood to say our goodbyes, it was as if the sun had suddenly burst through the clouds, because Mam would give Dr. Adamson one of her heart stopping smiles. The wonderful smile which said, 'Don't worry doctor, I'll keep on doing my best for her.'

With the passing years came the realisation that my cerebral palsy and all that it entailed, had the power to shrivel and destroy my existence if I were to let it. It was indeed all up to me. It was going to be an on-going battle – a battle that only I could fight. Only I could overcome this disability of mine – only I could throw in the towel, and I knew in my heart of hearts that I would never be able to do that. After all, I had hidden troops on my side.

I had Mam's love and constant care to soothe me and I had Dad's laughter and quick wit to lift my spirits so what more could I possibly ask for? Everything I needed was very close at hand.

And look at me now, nearly fifty years later. Still fighting and battling my way through life and still revelling in the daily achievements that it brings me. Yet who would have believed, during those long discouraging interviews with Dr. Adamson, that one day I would be 'pumping iron' in a health club? Well, not exactly 'pumping' it you understand – more like teasing it around it a little.

Dear Lord,

Thank you for the potential that each bright new day brings us and for the challenges that drop through our letterboxes to give new impetus to the routine of our everyday lives.

You know as well as I do Lord, that each new challenge has the power to raise our spirits and boost our self confidence and that more often than not, it brings with it the promise of a whole new circle of friends.

Help us to giggle at our shortcomings and to shout joyfully about our triumphs, but most of all Lord, give us the courage to grasp the nettle occasionally and prove to ourselves just how tough we really are. Amen.

A freezing dip in the North Sea

THE OPEN ASPECT

If your life, like mine, is distorted by pain, then you'll know how essential it is to have a dream, an ambition.

Little by little I can feel my strength ebbing away from me and it's a pity because there's still so many things that I want to do, countless places that I would love to visit... My dreams are so important to me that on the wall above my desk I have one of those cork board affairs and on it I pin all manner of glossy pictures and newspaper cuttings. I call it my 'Board of dreams'.

I'm gazing at it now as a matter of fact and if you were here beside me and we were looking at it together, I couldn't blame you if you giggled and said, 'Oh Lynda, what a strange mind you have.' Because in a way, you would be right. There's a whole jumble of thoughts and aspirations buzzing around inside this head of mine – a real mixed bag of wishes – and I suppose it's really these day-dreams and wishes that make up the inner part of me, the part which no-one ever sees.

I understand only too well the reason why some people feel the need to wrap their dreams up in tissue paper and hide them away. Rather like the tea set that we all have – the one collecting dust in our china cabinets – it's as if by lifting it out and using it, we may somehow cause it to shatter. Well just like those tea sets, our dreams are very fragile things too. They're easily damaged by hasty words and cynical smiles.

I've learnt from experience that disabled people, such as myself, aren't encouraged to have any burning ambitions in this life. For us, planning and dreaming of the future is usually frowned upon. We're urged to keep our hopes and our aspirations restrained, so that like damp squibs, the excitement and anticipation will one day peter out in them. Yet surely the dreams and aspirations of disabled people are just as valid, just as important, as everyone else's – they're just that little bit further away from us that's all – they need to be worked for just that little bit harder.

Shall I tell you about some of the pictures that I have pinned to my 'Board of dreams'? You never know, there may be a couple of dreams that we can dream about together?

There is a picture of a Norwegian log cabin … One day I'd love to wriggle my toes beside the blazing hearth of an isolated log cabin and to see through an open window, the view of a beautiful fjord.

There's a picture of a small squat thatched cottage…. I know it's naughty but one day I'd like to pick a bunch of wild flowers and to place them ever so lovingly on my own cottage window sill.

There's a postcard from Austria… One day I'd love to hold my breath during a cable car ride and yodel my way up some Tyrolean mountain.

I'd love to sail across the sea to Skye, tread softly across the bridge of Sighs, and waltz my way round and around in some gilded ballroom in Vienna.

I can't think of anything more exciting than of watching a ballet at Covent Garden or listening to an opera in Milan, except perhaps shouting "Yee Ha," at the Grand Ole Oprey or waving a Union Jack at the outrageous last night of the Proms!

Will I ever taste the intoxication on the centre court at

Wimbledon I ask myself, or smell the delicious fragrances at the Chelsea Flower Show? Well maybe not... I only know that my dreams have the power to blot out the pain on the days when my spirits sink low and isn't that precisely what daydreams are supposed to do?

But let's not forget these are only daydreams – they're nothing serious. My world won't suddenly crumble beneath my feet should they never happen to come true. Yet saying that, wouldn't it be wonderful if a few of them did!

I don't know about you, but I rarely pray for exciting things to happen. I tend to keep my prayers and my dreams in two very separate compartments in my heart. I have this theory that dreams and ambitions need to be struggled for and that prayers are quite a different issue altogether – they're quite above and beyond the powers of our control. I like to think that once a prayer has been uttered, that it floats like some perfumed balloon into heaven.

However, a long time ago, I did happen to have a dream that went hand in hand with a prayer. I made no secret of it, and I'm sure that everyone, who knew and loved me, prayed for it to happen too.

Come and sit beside me on this park bench. We'll close our ears to the sound of the traffic in the background and I'll tell you how it felt, for a brief time at least, to be walking down a road with an open aspect.

It wasn't until I reached junior school that I began to realise what a strong competitive streak I had within me and because I couldn't express this enthusiasm through any physical or verbal activity, I began to channel every ounce of energy into my everyday lessons at school. The stimulation which I found in the classroom gave my brain the kick-start that it needed and it fired in me an intellect which I hadn't known I possessed. It didn't take me long to realise that only through gaining and retaining knowledge could my true satisfaction

57

in life be achieved, and dare I say it, for a little while at least, I found myself walking down a road with an open aspect.

I wallowed and thrived in my studies, forever trying to prove that I was equally as clever as my friends, but sadly when I was placed top of my class, the strain proved to be too much for me and I began to have little fits in my sleep. These fits didn't last very long thank goodness, and I don't think they occurred too often, but they must have disturbed me greatly because I can still remember how alarming it felt when one of these attacks jolted me from my pillow. It was at times such as these that my Mam would ask the chemist to make me up a 'bottle', and whatever he put in it – phenobarbitone I think – well this seemed to calm me.

It was also about this time that I remember falling madly and shyly in love with my teacher, Mr Carr. I know that every child is capable of loving but the adoration that I felt for Mr Carr was different from any other feeling that I had known. It was an emotion which thrilled me through and through and I found myself liking the sensation.

For me there has never been and there never will be, any half measures where love is concerned and the school girl crush that I had on Mr Carr was the first indication of this. In my young mind he could do and say no wrong. He epitomised my ideal male. He was tall and slender, intelligent and kind and thinking back it seems that he had all the attributes a man needed to capture my heart.

I suppose we can all recall the people who have influenced our lives, simply by their example and I don't know about you, but I firmly believe that these people cross our paths for specific reasons. Mr Carr was definitely one of these special human beings. I can't say that he ever favoured me in any way, or that he gave me any preferential treatment, but I sensed that here was someone who was prepared to stand on my side, and I'll always be grateful to him for lighting the blue touch paper to my heart. It proved to me, even at the tender age of eleven, that no matter how awkward or strange my outward appearance might be, that my heart was indeed dancing to the right rhythm.

Another thing I had little control over was my infectious giggle – it caused me no end of embarrassment – and thinking back, I seemed to spend as much time sitting in the school corridor as I did sitting in the classroom and I'm going to blame my upbringing for this, because I was taught by Mam and Dad to see the funny side of every situation.

According to Anne, my friend, it was during our needlework classes that I caused her the most annoyance and frustration. Apparently I never allowed her to get on with her own sewing because I was forever pleading with her to thread and re-thread my needle.

I was a school prefect would you believe. A prefect, wearing a prefect's badge. Come to think of it, that prefects badge must have been the only vestige of authority that I have ever held. I really wish that I'd been allowed to keep it. I would love to hold it in my hand today and see for myself, the proof. I would run my fingers along its smooth yellow surface.... So once upon a time I did have self-confidence. Where is it now I wonder? Where along my journey did I loose it? And more importantly, who stole it from me?

Getting back to Junior School... I've always smacked my lips at the thought of a challenge so when the time came for me to sit my eleven plus examination, I was excited at the prospect. An extra year of preparation was offered to me but I stubbornly refused. Somehow it seemed wrong not to take my chance with the rest of my pals – No way were they going to leave me behind.

With Anne, I still played in the street, still enjoyed my childhood, but most of our leisure time was spent happily revising. We talked incessantly about the big brown envelopes which would one day drop through our letterboxes. The envelopes that would contain the news that we so desperately wanted to hear.

Anne and I were lucky in that we had the sort of parents who encouraged us with our school work and who went out of their way to provide us with the books which were so vital to our studies. I remember how it would only take one question – one query – to send Anne's Dad delving into the cupboard at the side of his chair. Out would come the dictionary, the encyclopaedia or the book of maps – he was that sort of person – and although he is no longer here with us, his kindness still lingers in my memory.

The Grammar school and all it promised, was very important to me. It stood like a shining beacon in my eye and it held the golden key to everything that I desired most in life. My eyes were set on it. My heart was fixed on it. I felt it to be the only goal worth striving for and I was determined to reach that finishing line, triumphant and proud. I had visions of myself holding the trophy up high, just like the champions did at Wimbledon. Yes I was certain that one day: success would surely be mine.

Dear Lord,

Thank You for the teachers who stride into our classrooms at precisely the right moment to take fresh command of our young people's minds. Make them aware of the huge responsibility that lies so heavily upon their shoulders.

Give each new generation of teachers a strong sense of purpose and a generosity of spirit, but most of all Lord, bless them with the ability to make the children around them feel special. Amen.

THE DESERTED BACK STREET

Last night, because there was nothing particularly interesting on the television, I reached for a video that had been given to me as long ago as last Christmas. It was a video celebrating Cliff's brilliant and successful career in show business.

After programming the video recorder, I settled myself deep, deep in an armchair, and with my arms wrapped tightly round a plump, agreeable cushion, I waited for Cliff to be miraculously transported into the cosy living room beside me.

Every warm winning smile from Cliff on the television screen prompted an echoing smile from me and before I knew it, I had this big soppy grin which had spread itself all across my face.

It amused me to find that my heartbeat still quickened at the sight of him, and that at the sound of his voice, my tummy could start tumbling and churning, just as it had done a hundred years before, and within minutes I was reliving all over again, those first innocent stirrings of adolescence. I was experiencing once more, that shivery shuddery stage of my life – when my teenage years had cruelly swept aside the final remains of my happy childhood.

In my youth I had simply adored Cliff, and last night, with only the fire light for company, I somehow managed to shed the trappings and the disguise of a middle-aged woman and imagined myself to be a young girl again. A young girl who was convinced that in the whole wide world, only she possessed that secret ingredient that could make Cliff happy. He had captured and secured a tiny piece of my heart then, and as I watched him on the television screen last night it became apparent that that piece of my heart was still his, and would remain his, always.

Long before the video had ended, I found that I had this huge lump inside my throat and bright shiny tears beneath my eyelids. (Is it only me, or do you feel sudden tears like this?) And it occurred to me that I owed Cliff an enormous debt of gratitude for helping me through one of the most difficult and painful periods of my life. And I came to the conclusion that although the memory of those teenage years remained tender and sore for me, Cliff and Cliff alone had made them oh so special – just as he must have done for countless other young girls of my generation. With his foot-tapping, hand-jiving music he had unknowingly kept me afloat...

Even today, if there was just one celebrities hand that I could hold for just a minute, then it would be Cliff's, and I would whisper just one single word – Thank you.

As we pass by this old decaying theatre, which once rocked to the music of Cliff and the Shadows, let's do a bit of hand-jiving together, and then, once we've finished giggling, I'll lead you down a back street which is hauntingly deserted.

I emerged from the eleven plus examination a borderline case, and a few days after receiving the disappointing news, I was summoned to a meeting in the head master's study. Naturally, my Mam came with me to provide the moral support that I so obviously needed, and in silence we listened as an official from the Education Department told us of their final decision. It had been decided that because of my cerebral palsy, a Grammar School education was thought to be out of the question.

Believe me, nothing in the past had caused me so much hurt and devastation, yet I knew deep down that it would be simply futile to argue my case. If ever there was a moment in my life when a clear voice was needed, it was then, in that room… Who gave this dignified stranger the right to determine my future I wonder?

I remember walking away from the head master's office, acutely aware that I was leaving all my hopes and all of my ambitions behind me. I had hoped to become a librarian but I knew then and there that my formal education was as good as over. There was to be no new challenges waiting for me at the school where I was heading – 'O' levels were non-existent.

September came and I was parted from my contemporaries. They went one way, wearing their smart red and grey uniforms and I was forced to go the other. It felt as if I'd been netted from a fast flowing stream and that my childhood companions had been allowed to swim on…

Of course I stayed in touch with my friends. No-one, not even the big-wigs on the Education Board could deny us our friendship and night after night I would sit beside them as they backed their new exercise books and spoke their first few words in French, and all the time I hurt, I really hurt.

At my new school I had no alternative but to make the most of my changed situation and soon a new circle of friends embraced me. Girls with fun on their minds. They were destined to become shop girls, office girls, factory girls, but never librarians….

Gradually, as the months passed, I found myself swapping my text books for the company of a small portable record player and together with my new found friends, I swooned my way through adolescence. Naturally I still enjoyed my work at school but my heart wasn't really in it any more. It belonged completely and absolutely to Cliff by now.

Believe it or not, I never had a conversation with a friend of the opposite sex for the next four years. The boys were taught separately at my new school and a high red brick wall kept us apart in the playground, and whenever I did happen to pass the boys by, I was either ignored by them or used as a figure of fun, someone to be taunted and laughed at. Their nasty remarks still echo ominously in my mind even today. They seemed to strip me of any sensuality that I may have had and they left me feeling completely wretched.

Without doubt this was one of the most hurtful periods of my life and I can still remember how every day I would walk the long way home from school – down deserted back streets – to avoid any actual contact with boys. Yet I longed for a wolf whistle… I would have given anything for a wolf whistle.

Somehow I managed to hold on tight to my dreams by gazing up into the eyes of Cliff on my bedroom wall. It's funny, but he never called me names or made rude gestures to me. He just smiled and winked at me, fuelling my imagination.

The words that he sang reminded me constantly of all the fun that I was missing, yet there was something in his voice that lead me to believe that one day, I too would meet somebody special. He gave me hope.

I spent the next few years searching hopelessly for someone who looked exactly like Cliff. If he didn't have a dark brown quiff and didn't have eyes that twinkled, then he definitely didn't figure in my daydreams.

It was Cliff's voice that somehow managed to erase all the hurt that I was feeling and I don't think I could have felt him closer, had he been sitting or dancing in the darkened bedroom beside me.

Admittedly, it was my friends as well as Cliff who helped me through this turbulent time. I lived my life through their eyes. I enjoyed watching them as they flirted and dallied with the boys and foolishly I pretended that I too had a smile that teased and a pair of hips that swivelled.

Although none of my classmates had what you might call a steady boyfriend, they were pretty certain that one day they would marry – I couldn't be so sure. In fact I tried not to think about what the future held in store, and if Mam and Dad had any real fears for me, they never ever voiced them.

I was happy enough. I had my music to keep my spirits high, and as always, Cliff gave me the feeling that happiness was just around the next corner.

Dear Lord,

If I could have just one prayer answered tonight, it would be for everyone in the world to be made to feel truly loved, even if it was from just a photograph on a bedroom wall.

Seek out the unloved of this world Lord, wrap your arms around them and hold them close, because just like Your heart and mine, their hearts will sometimes need a little resuscitating too. Amen.

With my friends from Senior School

65

THE TRAFFIC LIGHTS.

One of the compensations of being disabled is that I never have to worry too much about making new friends – nice people find me! They seek me out and make themselves known to me and every time this happens, my heart sings.

For reasons known only to themselves, strangers seem to find the nature of my disability an interesting topic of conversation, consequently, over the years, I've grown used to acknowledging their smiles and to answering their questions. And the funny thing is, I don't really mind! I don't mind how much they dig and delve into my personal life – I've nothing to fear by being honest with them – and if they leave me knowing just that little bit more about the condition, cerebral palsy, then my blushes and my breathlessness will not have been in vain.

But between you and me I'm terribly shy when it comes to going somewhere unfamiliar – say to a new hairdresser's or to a shopping centre that I haven't been to before. I try to melt unobtrusively into the background because I should hate my presence to cause any embarrassment to anyone.

As you can imagine, the first few days of a holiday are always pretty stressful. I feel terribly jittery and nervous when I'm walking around a new hotel for the first time, yet before re-packing my cases, new friends have been made and new addresses have been proudly scribbled inside my address book. Oh yes, I've met some really nice people whilst I've been on holiday.

The people I like the best are the ones who look me straight in the face. The ones whose eyes are not afraid of meeting mine... You'd be surprised if I told you just how many people avoid making eye to eye contact with me. Are they so distressed by what they see?

I count myself lucky in that I have a close circle of friends, people with very different personalities, and from each one of these friends I'm able to draw strength of a different kind.

After all, it was my friends who brought normality into my life, right at the very beginning – in the playground. As children, they were intelligent enough to be aware of our differences and yet wise enough to know that our differences didn't matter. And now, as we saunter into middle age together, it's to these same trusty companions that I still reach out to for their comfort and support. And with a bit of luck, these friends will be with me to the very end of my life, each one having enriched and embellished my existence in their own individual way.

I'm not saying that our oldest friends need necessarily be our closest friends, but they are the people who are best qualified to say, "Come on now, you've survived worse times than these." They are the people who have witnessed our struggles and our triumphs, consequently they know exactly what we're made of, and more importantly, they know precisely what it takes to make us tick.

Talking of friends, have you noticed how we always seem to meet new friends at the most unusual places? And getting to know them is so exciting, isn't it? It's rather like opening up the pages of a new book.

Why is it, do you suppose, that hospital friendships are so readily formed? Could it be that when we're in hospital we don't hide our vulnerability? The shutters of self-defence seem to come rattling down. We talk to one another, we become close, and before we know it, two hands are being clasped and two hearts are being gelled.

Perhaps that's one of the best kept secrets in life – that where-ever there is vulnerability, there will be friendship....

I see that the traffic lights are on green, so why don't you and I link arms and cross safely to the other side of this road. Only then, when we're safely across, will I be able to tell you about a special friend of mine called Jennifer.

Jennifer was a real pal... A thoroughly good egg... A joy to be with... We'd known one another since our earliest days at infant school and I had always found her attitude towards my disability to be spot on. In fact it was only ever with Jennifer that I had a hair pulling, name-calling, finger biting, show down. In other words, we loved one another to bits.

Jennifer was one of those friends who eventually left me to go on to study at the Grammar School, but as I said in the previous chapter, no one, not even the 'big guns' on the education board had the power to shoot our friendship down.

When other friends had homework to do, Jennifer never seemed to have any – well not of any importance anyway – and if she did sometimes have a little studying to do, then she could always be persuaded to abandon it to spend an extra hour or two with me.

One evening, in the summer of '61, I remember persuading her to put her textbooks aside for a little while and join myself and another couple of friends on an outing to the fairground.

We'd all had a smashing time together, but for some reason – a reason I can't for the life of me remember – Jennifer decided to leave for home just a few minutes earlier than the rest of us.

When the time came for us to follow in her footsteps, we saw that a small crowd of people had gathered together on the corner of the busy road – right next to the traffic lights. There had been some sort of accident. As we got closer we saw the body of a young girl lying motionless amidst the teeming traffic. A young girl, covered in a strangers coat. It was Jennifer. For eight long days she lay in hospital, in a coma, but tragically she never regained consciousness.

Jennifer had been barely a teenager when the accident had happened. Her life had been stretching before her like some scarlet satin ribbon, but that ribbon had been cruelly cut, and Jennifer was gone. No more was she able to make me throw back my head with laughter…

I know you'll think this sounds silly, but I never pass through those traffic lights without thinking of her, and shall I tell you a secret, I never picture her lying on the ground dying. I see her lovely face, laughing, always laughing! Oh yes, that's the one thing I'm very sure of, Jennifer must be the most amusing angel in heaven.

I doubt if you'll understand what I'm going to say to you now, but I'm convinced that at those traffic lights, on the corner of that busy road, Jennifer must have left all of her good fortune to me. How else can I account for the wonderful things that have happened since her passing?

We often talked of writing a book together, Jennifer and I. She was going to write the poems and I was going to write the stories. So because Jennifer was one of the first people to encourage me in my writing, and was therefore instrumental to this autobiography, I've decided to include one of her poems for you to enjoy. So here it is…

Tests come at the end of every year,
Oh what a lot of swotting,

I'm tired of looking at exam sheets and
paper used for blotting.

You're not allowed to whisper
Or write messages to each other.
Oh to be a little child and to stay at home with Mother.

The first bell goes and oh dear me,
I have not finished yet.
Alas I'm not even halfway though,
how many marks do you think I'll get?

So teacher spare a thought for me,
When writing out a test card.
Ask any question that you wish,
but please don't make it hard.

Jennifer (aged 12yrs)

There's no doubt in my mind that our friends are the birdsong in life's garden. Each friend having their very own song to sing… And let's not forget that a new friend never needs an invitation into our hearts. They fly in at the time of God's choosing and if we're very very lucky they then build their nests and stay.

Dear Lord,

Thank You for the warm familiarity that we find in the company of our friends. When we're with them let our lips say the right words and our arms make the right gestures and when the time comes for us to say our goodbyes let them be in no doubt at all as to how much their friendship has meant to us.

Give us the ability to keep on making new friends Lord, so that where ever we are, whether we're waiting at a bus stop or standing in a supermarket queue, we can be the ones who turn to the people beside us and say a warm and a cheerful Hello. Amen.

Dear Jennifer

71

THE HUMPED BACK BRIDGE

Ten years ago, to this very day, something pretty wonderful was delivered to our house. Shall I tell you about it? Well I'd just finished washing up the dinner plates, and I was busy drying my hands on my pinny, when all of a sudden there was this thunderous banging on our front door. As usual my nerves went all of a quiver, but after peering round the curtains to see who it was who was calling, I saw to my surprise that it was a delivery man and in his arms he was carrying my brand new word processor.

I flung the door wide open to greet him, and then, after signing the sheaf of invoices which he had pinned to his clipboard, I waited in the hall until he went back to his van to collect yet another couple of large cardboard boxes. To tell you the truth, I was glad that I was alone in the house when my computer arrived because it was, for me, a very special occasion.

Rarely do I show any outward signs of excitement when I'm opening up parcels, but on this occasion, as I tore open the packaging and dived in head first amongst the hundreds of coloured polystyrene chips, I could barely contain my squeaks of delight. I bet my face was a picture! I felt like a child again with my hand buried deep in the bran tub at the Christmas bazaar.

I know I should have waited until someone was around to help me, but I couldn't – I couldn't help myself – and slowly but surely I managed to lift each valuable piece of equipment from it's hiding place. Then somehow, don't ask me how, I carried the whole lot, piece by piece, up the stairs and into the little back bedroom where a place had already been cleared for it on my writing desk. It seemed heaven sent, coming at a time when I was finding it increasingly difficult to do the writing that I so much enjoyed.

Don't get me wrong, I knew that a computer wouldn't help me to produce better work – I knew that I would still have to struggle and search for the right things to say – and yes I knew that the words wouldn't come any faster or flow more eloquently, but at least when they did formulate in my mind, I knew now that my word processor would be there at my side to catch them for me and keep them safe.

Given time, I knew that I'd able to breathe a little life into it. I'd put a smile on its face, a giggle to its voice and a tune to its fingertips. I would give it a reason to print if only it would let me.

I'd nourish it with sincere thoughts and truthful information, so that in time it would have fire in its belly and passion coursing through its wires and only then, when it was all fired up and ready for action, would it be equipped to do the work for which it was intended.

That same night, as I sat facing the monitor for the first time, I asked the Lord for His help in enabling me to reach out the hand of friendship to His people everywhere. I knew that human beings, the world over, all needed a warm embrace from time to time and I desperately wanted to be those outstretched arms.

I must have got myself into a bit of a tizzy that night, what with all the excitement and everything, because when I did manage to tear myself away from the flashing screen and climb into bed, I couldn't for the life of me settle, so after tossing and turning on my pillow for an hour or more, I decided to tiptoe back into the study – just to make sure that the computer was still there and that I hadn't been merely dreaming about it.

We eyed one another suspiciously. We both knew that it would take time and effort on both our parts before we understood and trusted one another completely.

There it stood on my desk whilst I trembled nervously in my night-gown. Yes, it knew that it possessed a memory far greater than that of my own, and that as well as being able to correct all of my spelling mistakes, it boasted a strong right arm which could be persuaded to produce page after page of bold, dark print. No wonder this machine looked proud, it had clout. It possessed all of the qualities that I lacked and secretly I wondered whether we would ever become good friends.

One thing I was sure of, we needed each other. Apart, we were pretty useless, but I knew that once we shared the same objective in life then we were sure to become a very engaging pair.

Why don't you and I sit for a moment here on this humped back bridge, and then, when I've calmed myself down a little, I'll continue my story about my time at senior school.

I've always enjoyed writing and without sounding too big headed about it, I've always believed that I could weave a story line quite well. Maybe this confidence in storytelling stems from my four long years at secondary school and the close association that I formed with my English teacher, Mrs Skillern.

Mrs Skillern was a lady for whom I had a great deal of respect and admiration. Her delight for the written word was apparent and she communicated her knowledge with such charm and enthusiasm, that over the years I became completely and utterly captivated by her.

At a time when my self-esteem was at its lowest, it seemed as if Mrs Skillern singled me out and gave me that extra ounce of encouragement that I needed and like some kindly, fairy godmother she granted my dearest wish by suggesting that I became a school librarian. I was in heaven at last, surrounded by hundreds and hundreds of thick, dusty storybooks. I wanted to read them all – come to think of it, I think I did read them all!

Many happy hours were spent in that English room, working quietly and methodically, ensuring that every book was in its proper place and it gave me a great deal of personal satisfaction to know that in all the world, there couldn't be any other library shelves which were as neat nor as tidy as mine.

It was Mrs Skillern who, with gentle persuasion, encouraged me to learn the craft of the storyteller. I wrote to please her. I was hungry for her praise. Here was yet another teacher who believed in me.

"Lynda," she used to say to me, "one day you'll write a book of your own." And do you know, in a funny sort of way I believed her.

Time passed, and with Mrs Skillern's praise always ringing in my ears, I began scribbling in the backs of diaries and on thousands of scraps of waste paper until the time came when I didn't feel completely intact without a pen or a pencil in my hand. I even began working on a teenage romance, would you believe. I think I got up to about chapter eighteen or nineteen. I remember scribbling it all down in the best way that I could and then passing it across to my Mam who would rewrite every single word of it. She did so lovingly and willingly. Page after page after page…

Now, thanks to my computer, I've finally found my voice. The gag which has smothered my speech for so long has triumphantly been stripped away. Here at last is my very own bridge of communication. The vital channel through which my warmth and friendliness can flow freely into the world. Naturally I'm elated about it all and who can blame me and in the back of my mind I have this sneaking suspicion that there'll be nothing and no one who can stop me now!

Dear Lord,

Thank You for our talents. For the things that make us feel secretly good about ourselves.

Thank You for the people who come along from time to time to give us a shove in the right direction, but when the pushes come from You Lord, then we know that we are favoured indeed.

Give us the determination to succeed in life, and the courage of our convictions, and when set backs come, as they undoubtedly will, shout Your praise in our ears Lord, just that little bit louder. Amen.

Enjoying a book

THE SCENIC ROUTE

Alas, middle age has finally caught up with me! For the past couple of years I've been ducking and diving away from it and just when I thought I had it fooled, it's suddenly sneaked up behind me and triumphantly called out "BOO!"

That's exactly how it felt last Tuesday when I called in at the opticians to collect my very first pair of reading glasses.

It took me quite a while to realise that I needed some help in the eye sight department because like most people, if I spoke the truth, I'd been ignoring the problem. I'd been putting it down to lack of concentration whenever I tossed aside the morning paper after reading only a few leading paragraphs, and then it began to dawn on me – I was interested in only the front page because that was the page that was printed in bold type.

And in chapel it's been the same. I've been holding my hymn-book further and further away from me... So far away, that one Sunday evening I nearly knocked Addie's hat off. In case you're wondering who Addie is, she's a friend who sits with her husband Tom, in the pew in front of me.

The final straw came a couple of weeks ago when I was out shopping and I took a shine to a beautiful cream body warmer and matching jumper. In fact at the time I was feeling quite proud of myself because for once in my life, I didn't dither. I handed the items smartly over to the lady behind the cash desk, convinced that I'd just found the bargain of a life time and it was only when she asked me for eighty five pounds, instead of the thirty five pounds that I'd been expecting, that I came over all hot and bothered and muttered something about the colour not being quite right. Needless to say, I flew with it, like a mad woman back to it's rail and it was then, at that moment, when I knew for certain that I needed some specs. I make a fool of myself often enough without adding to my misdemeanours.

It was a bit of a pantomime though, having my eyesight tested. I found myself making several apologies for my wobbling head. I could feel it jerking around on my shoulders like some naughty marionette, and during the course of the examination I couldn't help but feel a great deal of sympathy for the lady optician because I knew that my unsteadiness was making her job extremely difficult for her. But like all professional people, it didn't seem to bother her too much.

After reading through the miniature letters on the wall chart, I was relieved to find that my eyesight wasn't really too bad at all. It was in fact, far better than I'd ever expected. And as I sat there, waiting for the optician to finish writing up her notes, I began to feel very grateful. I knew only too well that my cerebral palsy could have quite easily damaged my eyesight but it hadn't, and because of this I felt very fortunate indeed. I may not be able to voice clearly the beauty that I see, but at least I have the ability to see it!

So now, here I am, the proud owner of a pair of tortoise shell glasses. Well they're not exactly tortoise shell of course – they're more of a brown plastic – but wow, aren't spectacles a wonderful invention? I still can't believe the difference they make! And doesn't it feel great when you put them on and immediately you can see the writing that's right in front of your nose.

I must admit though, mine are a bit of a nuisance. For instance I go upstairs to bed and just as I bend down to pick up my bedtime reading, I find that I've left my glasses downstairs on the kitchen table. Or else I turn to the crossword puzzle in the morning paper only to find that, you've guessed it, my glasses are upstairs on the floor at the side of the bed. But never mind, maybe one of these days I'll get round to buying myself one of those sparkly spectacle chains that will dangle around my neck... Now then, that will be a blinking nuisance.

What are my eyes trying to tell me do you think? Are they warning me that they're growing tired, like the rest of my body? Are they reminding me of how hard they've worked for the past fifty-five years? After all, they've read, they've watched, they've cried, they've searched, they've found...

Because it's such a lovely day, why don't we deviate from our path for an hour or two and spend a little time out here in the countryside. Hang on, could I just borrow your glasses for a minute or two, just to read this map, because you know what I'm like, I've gone and left mine on the kitchen table at home.

Now according to this map, there should be a footpath just beyond this wooden stile, so come on, we'll each give the other a leg up and then we'll be ready to take the scenic route.

I don't know about you, but my idea of comfort is to snuggle beneath the blankets with a cup of hot milky Horlicks, a couple of digestive biscuits and a book that begs me to read on and on.

For some reason I need to be very quiet when I'm reading, therefore whenever I get the chance, I creep up the stairs as early as possible, have a lovely long soak in the bath and then climb into bed for a blooming good read.

All my life it seems as if I've devoured books as greedily as a child devours chocolate – I used to read anything and everything – no book was ever hidden away from me, and because they were all there on the book shelves in the living room, I was able to read them over and over again to my hearts content.

In my early teens, the library was about the only place that I was allowed to walk to by myself because there was only one major road for me to cross, and I remember how I used to return home from the library, breathless and happy, clutching Mam's large canvas shopping bag which bulged with books of all sizes and descriptions.

My Mam, who also shared my love of reading, used to belong to a book club, which I should imagine was quite a luxury in those days, and it was one of these books which, after reading it, had a lasting and powerful impact on me.

It was written by Elizabeth Goudge, and told the story of a family who abandoned life in the city to live deep in the heart of the countryside.

I was thirteen when I first read this book, a very impressionable age, and living in the industrial Northeast of England, you can imagine just how far away the countryside seemed to be for me.

Nature trails, up until then had consisted of walks, with my class mates, along side a disused railway track, or if we were extremely lucky, we were taken by bus to a nearby park. But even there in the park, the menacing backdrop of industry could be seen in the distance and I remember frowning at the dark depressing skyline, hating what I saw. I detested the stench and smoke that imposed itself upon me from every angle – suffocating me with its ugliness.

This book, 'The Herb of Grace', led me away from all that. It led me into a shimmering green world, where at every turn of the page, I would catch glimpses of rolling hillsides and prickly hedgerows and where, more often than not, scurrying animals would peep out at me from their secret habitats.

As if by magic, the writer led me by the hand, deeper and deeper into shady wooded glades where I could almost hear bird song overhead and feel the crispy dry brown leaves that snapped and crackled beneath my feet.

With her talented finger she pointed out to me the delicate wild flowers that nestled softly beside the soft mossy banks and trailed lazily beside the fast flowing streams until eventually I became desperate to visit the countryside to see if beauty such as this really existed.

Needless to say, after reading 'The Herb of Grace', my only dream was to live in a cottage in the country. It was to be a 'tea cosy' sort of a place, where small latticed windows would blink drowsily from beneath a thick heavy thatch. And where white muslin curtains would flutter like blonde eyelashes in the warm evening air. There was going to be a wide cheerful front door with a yellowing brass knocker, and inside the cottage, two sagging armchairs would almost sigh and bid you welcome. There would be a steep curving staircase that simply beckoned you to follow and everywhere, there would be that peace, that perfect peace that eludes us all.

Of course there would be a garden... Oh yes a garden that would intrude into the cottage as much as it dared. A garden where every kind of flower and shrub clamoured and jostled for attention... A place where climbing blooms would mingle with soft summer fruits to waft delicious scents to the busy bees and butterflies.

This garden was going to be my bit of heaven right here on this earth. A place of solitude... A place where a candy-floss sky would conspire with a huge yellow sun to give me day after day of sheer delight. A place where summer breezes whispered lullabies and where swaying trees danced in unison with all living things.

The obsession to own my own country cottage became so real to me that I even began to collect floral china and pretty plates.

Anything countrified, I would wrap carefully up in tissue paper and store gently away in a huge wooden tea chest.

Never once did Mam or Dad scoff at my plans when I told them of my intention to live in the countryside. They knew only too well just how much my ambition meant to me. And should they ever pass by my bedroom door and see me kneeling on the floor in front of my tea chest, they would simply smile and shake their heads, and leave me alone to dream my dreams.

Although my pretty things have long since been out of hiding, and are now placed here and there throughout my home, I can't help but feel that like me, they too are just that little bit disappointed that my country cottage never did become a reality.

But never mind, I still savour every day that I spend outside in the open air and whenever I see people striding a little too briskly down a leafy lane, I make sure that my feet meander even more slowly. No sight or sound escapes my notice. All the intricacies of nature I see and appreciate. But yes, if I'm truthful there'll always be a part of me that stays discontented and all because I opened up the front cover of 'The Herb of Grace'.

Dear Lord,

Just like the writer, Elizabeth Goudge, take hold of our hands and lead us deeper and deeper into the very heart of the countryside.

Once we are there Lord, help us to toss aside our cares and our worries for a little while and turn our tired eyes to the breathtaking beauty of Your natural world.

Awaken our appreciation and stimulate our senses, and then when our lungs are full to bursting, listen to our prayers Lord as we praise and glorify Your Holy name. Amen.

THE GRASS VERGE

I wonder, are you like me? Every September when you walk into your local library, are your eyes instinctively drawn towards all those neat little piles of pamphlets and leaflets – the ones promoting adult education? And does some force propel you, as it does me, to pick up each prospectus in turn, to scan its pages for some appealing invitation? Because that's really what each prospectus is, isn't it, a collection of cordial invitations?

I'm always tempted to try every course that's available to me, especially the ones, which declare themselves to be 'Especially for Beginners'. And before I've finished reading through each prospectus, my eyebrows are dancing up and down with anticipation and a little voice inside my head is beginning to whisper, "I bet you could do that".

When you come to think of it, there's no need for any of us to be sitting at home feeling sorry for ourselves, is there? Not with so many people out there who are only too willing to pass on their skills for our enjoyment…Why sit alone watching the telly, when we could be out there, twirling our skirts and knocking our knees with others in a Scottish country dancing class – well that's my philosophy!

But seriously, could you see me at a potter's wheel? No, neither could I. Imagine me tossing a pot! I could toss it all right – but where would it land, I ask myself… And I can visualise my creations now…

A vase that couldn't hold water and a cup that couldn't hold tea! But we'll never know what we can do until we give these things a try will we?

Here's a funny story for you. A few years ago I went along to our local comprehensive school with the sole intention of enrolling on a cookery course. 'Healthy eating', was how it was described in the prospectus.

The school hall was literally heaving with people when I arrived. All kinds of people. Some were there, eager to learn a new craft, others were there, keen to take up a new hobby, and who knows, maybe amongst the crowd there may have been one or two frightened people, frightened that the dark winter nights were about to shroud them in loneliness. In other words, they were people just like you and me.

As I say, the place was packed. There were queues everywhere. Queues waiting to fill in forms, queues were waiting to pay their fees. There were even queues to reach the queues, if you get the picture.

Anyway I made a blunder. I'm always making blunders of one sort or another but this one was a real corker! Somehow, don't ask me how, I managed to write down the wrong code number on my enrolment form, and I found to my horror that instead of enrolling for a cookery class, that I'd enrolled for a course in yoga instead.

I don't know about you, but I'm one of these people who just hate making a fuss – I'll go to any lengths to avoid causing a scene – so I walked away, or should I say I staggered away from the girl at the enrolment desk and plonked myself down on the nearest chair, feeling slightly dazed and extremely silly.

Yoga! I'd never given the subject much thought before, but I knew that the exercises would involve tying myself up in some very awkward positions, and then there would be all that weird chanting and OMMMMMMMMING to contend with... I remember saying to myself "What on earth have you done now?" as I stared down at the slip of paper in my hand. But it was no use crying over spilt milk. The dye had been cast, and to be honest with you, I simply hadn't the courage to retrace my steps and begin the rigmarole of explaining my dilemma to the young enrolment officer. So there was only one thing for it and that was to give the course in yoga a go.

The next day when I told Mam and Dad about the predicament that I was in, they simply said that they thought yoga was a wonderful idea and that maybe I wouldn't find the exercises as difficult as I imagined. I might have known what their reaction would be. I had gone to their house hoping for a bit of tea and sympathy but instead all I'd got was the usual jokes and laughter. And to add insult to injury, a couple of days later they bought me an exercise mat as an early birthday present, so I knew then that there was going to be no way out.

Eventually, the dreaded evening was upon me, so off I went, comforted by the fact that my baggy jogging suit was concealing at least some of my plumpness, but of course it wasn't, in reality my track suit wasn't hiding anything at all – my bulges still showed – and after entering the classroom and comparing myself to everyone around me, I saw that I was badly out of shape, extremely over weight and definitely out of condition – and that was before the exercising had begun!

Even my new exercise mat which lay on the parquet floor in front of me, looked pretentious and out of place. Everyone else, I noticed, had tatty bits of carpet or soft pieces of blanket to lay on, trust me to be the one with the 'deluxe' exercise mat! I remember cursing Mam and Dad beneath my breath and just prayed that I wouldn't be mistaken for the instructor.

The funny thing was, the teacher did have a mat that was identical to mine but that was where all similarities ended. She was a lady with a perfectly formed figure and a beautiful soothing voice.

That first night, as I lay on my 'deluxe' exercise mat, staring self-consciously up at the ceiling, I was re-introduced to my body for the first time in years, and between me and you I was appalled by what I found. The whole of my left side was shaking and juddering around like a skeleton with flu. It refused to keep still. And to make matters worse, there seemed to be nothing at all that I could do about it.

Eventually we were told by the teacher to listen to our bodies and to be aware of our breathing... It didn't take me more than a few seconds to realise that my body was that of an alien being, and as for my breathing, well it was extremely erratic and completely out of control.

It was only when the exercising was over and I was curled up once more on my red plastic mat that I really began to unwind and enjoy myself. Maybe it was the haunting music which calmed me, or perhaps it was the hypnotic voice of the teacher which cradled me to sleep... I don't know what it was, I only knew that I was hooked. I was ready to sign up to be a Buddhist monk, it felt so good. It was at this point in the evening when we were told to think of a place – a restful place. Somewhere where the sun shone. Somewhere where we felt absolutely at ease. Without any hesitation my mind swirled through the mists of time and came to rest in the quiet seaside town of Saltburn.

Come, lay beside me on this grass verge and as we lift our faces towards the sun, I'll tell you about the days when I used to think that factor twelve was a term used in maths, when I imagined the greenhouse effect to be a way of cultivating seedlings, and when I supposed the ozone layer to be something vaguely connected to the icing of cake.

My love affair with Saltburn began way back in my early child-hood and although the resort was just seven miles from the town where we lived, it seemed to me to be an incredibly long way away from home.

Mam and Dad had taken the advice of the paediatrician seriously when he had stressed the importance of fresh air and exercise for me, and as one hot summer succeeded another, they made sure that I spent lots of days playing and paddling on the windswept shores of the North Sea. The bracing air of Saltburn seemed to be the ideal place for strengthening my weak lungs and you would often find me on Saltburn beach, building large imposing sandcastles and soft and squidgy mud pies.

Saltburn beach was also the setting for our annual Sunday school trips and I can see us all now, sitting around in huge merry circles, juggling with thermos flasks and battered cake tins. It would only take a sudden shower of rain to send us all scuttling for shelter beneath the huge iron girders of the pier, and there we would stay until the shower had subsided. All of us giggling and gleeful, clutching our soggy egg and tomato sandwiches close to our chests. Come to think of it, the egg and tomato sandwiches that I make today don't taste nearly as good as they did then, with that sprinkling of sand for seasoning. Or maybe it was merely the company that made every aspect of those seaside picnics so memorable?

Inevitably, it was Saltburn where we chose to spend many of our family holidays. We would stay there for a week in the summer and if we were lucky, we would return in the autumn for another week's vacation. Mam and Dad always encouraged me to take my dollies pram with me on these holidays because they knew that it would help me to walk just that little bit further. And I think that's one of the earliest recollections that I have – of standing on the station   platform and watching Dad as he hoisted my dollies pram high into the guards van. It always seemed so dark in there that I used to   wonder whether I would ever see my doll and pram again.

When I was fourteen, because of all the happy associations that we had had with Saltburn, Mam and Dad decided to buy a caravan there and it was an incredible feeling to know that at last we had a permanent base beside the sea. Somewhere where we could stay for weekends and for large, fat chunks of the school holidays.

I remember as a teenager, how I used to lie on the short springy grass in front of the caravan. I'd have a small transistor radio close to my ear and a long cool drink of lemonade close to my elbow and I would spend hours - whole afternoons - just gazing up at the sky, with not a care in the world. This was long before the sun became a sinister thing. A monster to be avoided. This was when you could actually sit outside in a deck chair, dab a bit of suntan lotion on your nose and you didn't have to bother your head about the greenhouse effect or the ozone layer. Even suncream factors were hardly ever mentioned – you simply lay back and relaxed.

Once upon a time in Saltburn, at the sprawling feet of Huntcliff, a fairground used to attract crowds of young people and pop music used to dominate the air – wiping out even the sound of the gulls – and selfconciously I would lean against the gilded pillars of the Waltzers and be a part of the scene. Part of the scene and yet not part of the scene if you know what I mean. I was never included.

There was also a very old and dilapidated cinema in Saltburn in those days, and once or twice a week in the summertime, I would drag my Nana along to watch the colourful musicals of Cliff and Elvis. And although Nana used to moan and groan a bit about my choice of music – a Viennese waltz was more in her line – I have a sneaking feeling that she used to enjoy these outings far more than she ever let on. After watching the film we would then stroll back along the promenade to the caravan site, eating our fish and chips suppers straight out of their newspaper wrappings – the chips, I hasten to add, liberally sprinkled with salt. High cholesterol was yet another subject that was never ever mentioned.

I dreamed my dreams in Saltburn and as you travel with me through this journey of ours then you'll see that some of my dreams came true there.

In those hazy far off days, everyone staying at the caravan park seemed to wear happy, sun-tanned faces, and looking back, I can see now that this contentment had nothing whatsoever to do with possessing great wealth or wearing chic designer labels. It came from knowing that what we were tasting was good. It was called freedom. Yes, we had the bare essentials in life. We had fresh air, good appetites and good company and we had God's natural beauty all around us. No wonder we were all so delighted to be staying there. Especially the children, who romped and played amongst the caravans, whether in sunshine or in showers.

Now, forty years later, I find that there is still a healing quality about Saltburn that never fails to soothe the mind and refresh the spirit. Even the rain drops, I've noticed, have a way of falling ever so softly over the town, just as if they're all part of God's plan in keeping the place as tranquil and as restful as possible.

Can you guess where I'm writing this chapter? That's right, you've got it. I'm here at the caravan. It's rather quiet, immensely comforting, and it feels oh so good to be here.

Dear Lord,

Wouldn't it be wonderful if everyone with a troubled mind could be granted his or her very own deckchair in the sun? Somewhere

where they could escape to when the stresses and strains of everyday life became a little too much for them to bear?

It doesn't have to be on a foreign beach Lord, or in a paradise garden... It just needs to be in a secluded spot, somewhere where the wind refuses to blow.

So whether we take our ease on a garden bench or on a church pew, flood it with golden sunshine Lord, and let us feel the radiance or Your peace. Amen.

Happy carefree days

THE FORK IN THE ROAD

What a strange dream I had last night. I dreamt that I was in chapel and halfway through the evening service, the whole of the congregation suddenly rose to their feet and began discussing ways of making some money to boost the forever ailing church fund. All sorts of good ideas were being put forward – table top sales, car washes, strawberry teas, and without any hesitation, I shouted at the top of my voice that I would hold a coffee morning – one day when the weather was fine – so that we could all sit outside and sun ourselves in the seclusion of our back garden.

The minute the words were out, I regretted them. But don't get me wrong, it wasn't the coffee morning itself that I regretted, it was the fact that I didn't possess many cups and saucers. What I mean is I didn't possess many cups and saucers that actually matched.

The next thing that happened, David, the minister, was racing excitedly up the pulpit steps and announcing breathlessly in the microphone, "There's a coffee morning in Lynda's garden next Wednesday at 10am. Everyone's invited, but she's asked me to ask you, would you mind going along in twos."

Of course I panicked. Yes, even in dreams I manage to panic, and silently I started to bewail my impulsive behaviour – and of course my big mouth. Then with a face as red as a beetroot I began stammering my way through a whole string of lame excuses. What if I couldn't manage the pans? What if I didn't have enough chairs? What if...Naturally, every excuse that I mentioned was shouted down. "We'll give you a hand" – "We'll bring our own chairs" voices cried out all around me, but to be honest with you, it wasn't the lack of chairs or the pans of milk that were bothering me, I was thinking more about the cupboard where I kept my odd assortment of crockery and in my minds eye I could see all those old cups and saucers which were stacked up in there... All those cups with the hairline cracks around their rim. Not to mention the cups that hadn't any handles on them at all!

Come to think of it, that's the one distinctive sound you'll hear whenever you pass by our house and that's the sound of breaking glass – I'm simply hopeless! I even bought six unbreakable Pyrex beakers a couple of years ago and guess what – I managed to drop and break them all. But looking on the bright side, we've always got plenty of broken crockery to sit in the bottom of our plant pots!

So it isn't any wonder is it, that when Christmas morning comes along, I never find any bone china tea sets or any crystal wine goblets in the bottom of my Christmas stocking? I'm given serviceable items, like cast iron casserole dishes and thermal plastic teapots – the sort of things that it would take a flipping sledge hammer to break.

So don't forget, if you have any hideous wedding presents that you want to be rid of, just ask me to dust them for you a couple of times, and whoops... before you know it, they'll be a distant memory.

But seriously, now I come to think of it, my hands have always caused me problems of one sort or another. They seem to do their own thing, if you know what I mean. This clumsiness of mine never seemed to be too much of a problem for me when I was at school – I must have muddled my way through somehow – it was only when

I started to look for employment that I began to realise just how much my hands were going to let me down.

We have before us a fork in the road. Shall we venture left or right? One signpost points to a pathway that is rugged and steep and the other signpost indicates a footpath that is much, much easier... Which path shall we choose, do you think? Oh come on, let's be daring and take the high road, because as I said at the beginning of my story, the view will be well worth the climb.

How well I remember shedding tears during the singing of the school hymn as my friends and I stood together for the final assembly of our school days. Whether my tears were for the past or for the future, I'm really not quite certain, I only know my tummy turned violent somersaults whenever I thought about the challenges that lay ahead.

Was it foolish of me to believe that there was a place for me beyond the safe secure perimeter of the school walls? I didn't think so. To be honest with you, I'd had my belly full of learning and I was ready for the first time in my life, to confront my future, head on.

Mam and I had already been to see the school careers officer and together we had learnt of all the jobs that he thought were beyond my capabilities – as if we needed to be told. It was infuriating to know that my mind was capable of comprehending so many skills, yet my hands were going to prove useless in implementing them.

I was advised by the career's officer to accept the 'green card' which was on offer to me. It was to be my passport to a life of ease...A life of boredom. But how on earth could I accept it? My independence was at stake here, and in my book, my independence had always been something well worth fighting for. Obstinately I rejected their green card. I felt that I hadn't struggled so far in life only to be categorised as worthless.

Luckily, my stubbornness paid off and I was extremely grateful when a friend of my Dad's managed to find a clerical position for me with an engineering firm in Middlesbrough, and looking back, I can see now that my adult life began the moment that I walked through the polished swing doors of their office block.

After being led into the typing pool and being introduced to the typists, I was shown the work which I was to do for the next seven years. It was a tedious and undemanding job, checking one invoice with another – any fool could have done it – but I would have willingly pushed the tea trolley around the corridors, just for the privilege of being there.

Within a matter of weeks I felt completely at home, facing no prejudice or discrimination whatsoever, and as the months and years slipped effortlessly by, I was accepted by my work mates with friendliness, and in time, affection.

Being a working girl wasn't without its problems though, especially in winter, when snow and ice made mobility for me almost impossible. I remember how Mam would beg a lift for me from everyone and anyone that she could think of. Her pride always came secondary to my wellbeing, and sometimes, when no car was available to take me into town, she herself would take me into Middlesbrough on the bus, and then, with her usual optimism, carefully navigate me through the snow. Don't get me wrong, the journey wasn't really that dangerous or hazardous, but to Mam and I it felt as if we were competing in the prestigious winter Olympics.

After making sure that I was safely inside the office block, Mam would then return home, ready to begin her own day's work as a rent collector. Never once did I hear her complain or ask for gratitude, my happiness and safety was all that really mattered to her and often I would marvel at the sheer force of energy which exuded from her.

It was as if the Lord had blessed her with enough vitality for the two of us, and that he had given me the humility never to take her love and help for granted.

In the office, I was never awarded the promotion that I deserved, but so what, I had the thing which mattered most to me – companionship. And there was always so much laughter and girly gossip to be enjoyed, and of course plenty of tea breaks that were filled with idle chit-chat.

When I was sixteen I had my first real date and because there was a sprinkling of snow on the ground, can you guess who came with me? That's right... My Mam! I'd arranged to meet the lucky fellow at the bus terminal in Middlesbrough and this suited me fine because it meant that if my date was there then I could jump off the bus without my Mam being seen and if he wasn't there, then I could just stay on the bus and make the return journey home.

My date was there, I'm pleased to say, waiting to take me to the pictures, where, I hasten to add, he sniffed loudly all the way through the film. Okay, so it wasn't exactly the kind of date that dreams are made of, but it was good enough for me and for the next week or two, as you can imagine, my ego was terribly inflated.

My friends in the office coaxed me into a pulsating, vibrant world. They took me into discos where coloured lights flashed, they led me into ballrooms where huge silver spheres sparkled, and as the years passed, and we grew more confident and at ease in one another's company, we ventured into smoke filled night-clubs where saxophones screamed lazily into the early hours of the morning.

Often I would crawl home to bed, happy and exhausted, only to be awakened at seven o'clock the following morning by my Mam, who had a fire blazing in the hearth and bacon sizzling in the pan, ready for my breakfast. This must have been an extremely worrying time for her and Dad. They never really settled until they knew that I was home safely, and when I look back, I can see now, that it would have been the easiest thing in the world for them to keep me safe and secure at home with them. But they didn't. Somehow they had found the courage to set me free.

Of course there were evenings of pain. Nights when I would be openly mocked and criticised by young men who would say quite openly to my friends, "Why do you hang around with her?" The replies were always whispered…Naturally, hurtful remarks such as these used to cloud my evenings and I would return home to Mam, vowing never to set foot in a discotheque again, yet the following Saturday evening you would find me all dressed up in my usual finery, dancing in my own peculiar fashion beneath the spinning mirrorball.

Boyfriends were few and far between I remember, and more often than not, after just a few dates, they would be kind enough to say, "Sorry Lynda, I like you but I could never love you." Don't get me wrong, I always appreciated their honesty, but time and time again I used to wish that they had taken just a bit more time to get to know me a little better.

Now and again some joker would take me home from a dance, hoping that because of my disability, they would find me an easy target, but before the evening was over he would have been firmly put in his place and left with no doubt at all as to the sort of girl I was.

I was as innocent at twenty-one as I had been at fifteen, but just like the rest of my friends, I knew what my heart had to offer to that special boyfriend who would one day come along.

Mam used to say, "Somewhere, there is someone for everyone," and I, naïve as I was, used to believe her. Yet true enough, he came, but that's another story.

Dear Lord,

When the time comes for us to make our way in this big wide world, help us to choose the right path. The path which is right for us.

Don't let us be fooled by the signpost that points to an easy footpath because You and I both know Lord that an easy footpath will probably lead us nowhere. And once we're on a flat and easy footpath we soon realise that it has very little to offer us in the way of thrills and excitement.

So please Lord, whenever we approach a fork in the road, give us a nudge in the right direction, and then when the going gets tough and the terrain gets a little bit steeper than usual, give us the tenacity to climb to great heights. Amen.

With my friends from the office

THE UNEXPECTED TURNING

I wonder if you share my enthusiasm for jigsaws! I've always been a bit of a glutton for them myself. The more pieces the better. But although I say it myself, this latest jigsaw of mine has proved to be a bit of a nightmare. It's been a bit too much for me to handle if I spoke the truth, and there was a moment, just a couple of days ago, when I thought that I was never going to finish it at all. I bought it way back at the beginning of August, at the annual Red Cross jumble sale.

Have you ever stood in a jumble sale queue, waiting for the front doors to open? It's an experience that shouldn't be missed. Everyone in the queue gives the impression of being so amenable and friendly. They stand around chatting idly to one another about the weather and the latest offers at the Co-op, but believe me, the moment those front doors fly open, it's as if suddenly, everyone takes on a different guise. They become like green eyed Honey monsters, pushing and shoving. And no matter how close I am to the front of the queue, you can bet your bottom dollar that when the time comes for the Grand Opening, I'm always the last one to stagger through those gaping front doors. And then when I do eventually pull myself together and find my bearings, I marvel as to where everyone else has sprung from. By this time, every table is usually surrounded by a heaving scrum of potential rugby players… I always think that it would be a good idea to have a paramedic on duty at jumble sales, and if possible, an ambulance ready and waiting outside of the front door.

Only once have I tried to elbow my way through a jumble sale crowd and believe me, it wasn't worth the effort! I finished up with my legs quivering in mid air… So these days I tend to wait until the real crush is over before I even begin to browse around the tables. I may miss out on the odd bargain from time to time but at least this way I emerge from the jumble sale relatively bruise free.

So what is it about jumble sales that brings out such aggressiveness in otherwise quiet and submissive people? Perhaps they anticipate finding some priceless antique amongst the bric-a-brac? Or some invaluable masterpiece? I don't know what it is, I only know that there's never any objet d'art or any Ming vases at the jumble sales that I go to, but every once in a while I do unearth a something of a treasure – like this jewel of a jig-saw for instance.

I don't know about you, but I'm simply hopeless once I have a jigsaw puzzle on the go. I can't pass it by without popping in a piece or two, and then my back aches, so I sit down, and this of course proves fatal. I forget the time, I forget the pans on the cooker, and it's only when I smell burning that I jump up and shoot off back into the kitchen. Perhaps jigsaws should come with some sort of government health warning on the box – something like, 'Only open this box if your spring cleaning is finished' or 'Do not attempt this jigsaw if you are preparing a meal.' And who knows, perhaps this would prevent a few house fires from being started, and maybe more lawns would be mowed and more dust would be scattered?

I was a bit disappointed yesterday though, because although this latest jigsaw puzzle of mine was taking shape nicely, I had the distinct feeling that there was going to be a piece or two missing. And there's nothing worse is there, than spending day after day reconstructing a beautiful picture, only to find that the picture you are working on can never be completed?

As I say, I'd spent literally hours idling my time away on this latest jig-saw puzzle and I was at that crucial moment when I had only a few more pieces to slip into place. And you know what it's like, the closer you are to completing the picture, the faster it is to pounce on the right piece…Well there I was, popping the pieces in like crazy, but alas my instincts were right – there was definitely a piece missing.

We have before us, an unexpected turning. Let's find out where it leads us, shall we?

Every time I watch Cilla Black introducing 'Blind Date' on the television, I have a little chuckle to myself and reminisce about the one and only blind date that I ever went on.

It happened when a friend from the office invited me to join her and her boyfriend for an evening at a local nightspot. Secretly she had arranged for her boyfriend to bring along a partner for me and after learning about their well-intentioned matchmaking there wasn't a great deal that I could do about it, except to go along with the plans which had already been hatched. I suppose I must have been a bit nervous at the time but I seem to remember laughing and scolding them both and treating the whole affair as just a bit of a joke.

The moment I saw the two men together in the nightclub, I had a feeling that my blind date wouldn't be the tall, fair, pleasant-faced young man who was chatting so amicably to the crowd at the table. And I was right. My date was the other. A short, bespectacled, serious looking chap called John. But thanks to that meeting, so tenuous in it's making, my existence here on earth, was irrevocably changed overnight.

It was his name that first caught and held my attention – Gallilee – such an unusual name, yet to my ears, it conjured up for me many

100

colourful and heart warming pictures. Something stirred inside me the moment I heard it and I wanted to know more about this man called Gallilee. I wanted to know what kind of man he was. I wanted to know what made him tick. And that was really how our love affair began – with a simple shake of the hands. And I suppose that's the way that most love affairs begin when you come to think of it...

Good things happened from the moment we met. Our hands touched within hours, our arms entwined within weeks and before only a few months had passed, our hearts had become almost inseparable. At last I had someone of my very own to share some secret smiles with.

Very early in our courtship John and I knew that we were destined to be together always... Don't ask me how we knew. We just did. It was as if all the angels in heaven had conspired together to make it so. Why else could it be that my hand fitted so neatly into his and our hearts beat in unison to the same rhythm.

I don't know what was being whispered behind the cupped hands of our families and friends, I only knew how it felt whenever John walked into the room and the minutes that we spent in one another's company became very precious indeed.

I can't begin to tell you how wonderful it felt to have found a friend who was so true. It was as if the whole world had suddenly become a different place. Everything felt so vibrant and new. People and places didn't swim before my eyes any more. Even the ground beneath my feet became more solid and reliable.

Every kind word from John irradiated at least a thousand cruel jibes from the past and eventually, I found to my surprise, that his kind and gentle manner had swept the memory of them all clean away.

Gradually I came to understand the meaning of the word 'love'. I began to realise what people meant when they wrote about it in stories and sung about it in songs. It was as if every romantic novel that I had ever read and every soppy love story that I had ever watched at last made sense. John became my reason for living.

As the weeks and the months whipped dizzily by, I delighted in taking John to my favourite places. I took him to Saltburn, to the caravan site. I showed him the chapel. He felt at home there. Proudly I introduced him to the people in my life, the people who really mattered, and shyly and unobtrusively he became part of the family.

He became the brother I'd never had. He became the lover I'd never had. His kind and loving ways gradually brought out the best in me. They brought out the courage in me. The pride in me. The faith in me. And I'm convinced that it was due entirely to John's love that I was able to unravel my tangled thoughts and bury them deep, and fix my eyes firmly on the future.

Seven months after our meeting John proposed to me and I'd like to be able to tell you that the proposal was a romantic affair. That it was an evening of wine and roses. But of course it wasn't. It was just a conversation between a boy and a girl. A boy and a girl who were very much in love, I suppose it was just the natural progression of things really…

In our tender moments we talked about the future that we were going to share together and believe me, the dreams that we wove in each other's arms weren't those of a flimsy kind. They were brick solid. And with these precious bricks of hope we constructed our very own castle of dreams.

One day I remember taking John to meet Polly. Sadly, she was very ill at the time but I was determined that John should meet her. It was terribly important to me that John should meet the lady who had loved me, loved me so unconditionally, just as I had loved her. And it was strange because soon after John and I became engaged, Polly told a relative, "I've had a lovely dream – The Queen has given our Lynda a beautiful diamond ring."... So you see, perhaps Polly really did know all there was to know about John after all.

Yes, John was definitely the missing jigsaw piece in my life and once he had appeared in the picture, my life at last became complete.

Dear Lord,

Thankyou for the unexpected turnings that we sometimes take and for the people who bring instant happiness into our lives when we least expect it. It is You, isn't it Lord, who sends them to us? Are our lives spread out before you like some gigantic multicoloured jigsaw puzzle? And like us, do you delight in popping in the right pieces?

Which ever way it happens, Thank You Lord, because without true love in our lives, our feelings of entirety would never be complete. Amen.

My Darling John

THE QUIET SIDE STREET

Believe me, my intentions were good yesterday morning as I struggled up the stairs with my Hoover and duster. I was going to 'break eggs with a stick.' But you know how it is, you open a drawer or a cupboard to put something away, and before you know it, all thoughts of cleaning are completely forgotten.

This is precisely what happened to me yesterday. It's as if I had been drawn to that cupboard almost, and no sooner did I open the door, did photographs, souvenirs, and pieces of paper come slithering out. Frantically I tried pushing them back into place again, but in the end I just gave in and let the whole lot tumble out around me. Then I smiled and realised that this was the Lord's way of telling me to simmer down and rest for a while, and take a little time to remember...

Gathering my assorted treasures close to me, I squatted down on the bedroom floor and allowed myself the luxury of looking back...

We all have a 'treasure chest' don't we? A private place, where we can go once in a while to relive again those magic moments. Some folk open their treasure chests in search of comfort or of peace. Others need to be reminded of happier times, or their eyes long to see again that well loved face, the face they miss so much.

Me – well I'll be honest with you, when I go hunting through my treasure chest, I go in search of encouragement – I go looking for that certain something that will spur me on. As you can imagine, I often get tired, and on the days when the stairs seem that little bit steeper than usual, and the Hoover feels that little bit heavier, I feel the need to clasp the Lord's hand and feel His soothing fingers entwined in mine…

So there I was, squatting down on the bedroom floor, examining every object which had fallen into my lap, and with each photograph and postcard that I touched, a new emotion swept through me. Gone was my aching back and anxious expression – I was basking in glorious memories.

At last my eyes found what my heart had been looking for – an old iron key. Lovingly I picked it up and held it tight. It represented so much happiness. It was the key that had opened the door to our very first home and it was given to us on the day that John and I became engaged.

You must be tired my friend, after all, we've travelled quite a distance! Just bear with me for a little while longer because there's just one more street that I really want you to see.

Can you hear the workmen whistling? They're busy with their hammers and their chisels and mingling with these sounds of activity you can almost hear a few whispers of excitement.

It's true that most of my days are happy ones, but the day of our engagement, I shall remember always. It was a strange experience for John and I to suddenly find ourselves in the full broad beam of the spotlight, but if the truth were told, the two of us revelled in our moment of glory. And it was a truly glorious moment when John slipped the diamond engagement ring onto my finger. It's just a tiny diamond – hardly worth a mention – but sometimes it astonishes even me with its capacity to sparkle in the darkest of places.

Getting back to that day in June … There were cards to open and presents to unwrap, and somehow within this whirlpool of excitement, we found ourselves the centre of attention at a party organised by our families and friends.

Later that night, when the flurry and the confusion of the day was over, and we were relaxing back at home with my Mam and Dad, my Mam handed us this key. As I've already told you, Mam was working at the time for a local estate agent, consequently she was often in the position of helping young couples find their first home.

Still you can imagine how surprised and delighted we were, and how eagerly we listened as she told us snatches about the little house. "It needs a lot of work doing to it," I can still hear her say, "and it's £600!" Could we afford it, we asked ourselves? Well maybe just!

There wasn't any peace until she promised to take us along to see it, so the following evening, after work, we went with her and Dad to view it. Somehow, the tiny house seemed to embrace us and John and I rejoiced in its hospitality. Yes, we decided to buy it and I am ever so glad that we did.

Never once did it occur to us that I could neither peel a potato nor scrub a floor – potatoes were the last things on our minds. We had our faith, our love for one another and the invaluable support of our parents, so how on earth could we falter?

It seemed to take months for all the paper work to be completed, but I remember as if it were yesterday, sitting quietly at my desk one summers afternoon, and being distracted by someone tap-tapping on the office window. I glanced up to see John's cheery face grinning at me above the frosted glass. He was dangling something high in his hand. It was this very key. It seemed that the house was finally ours.

I remember running outside to take the key from him and after hugging each other with tingling anticipation, off he went to do his afternoon shift at the swimming baths where he worked. I doubt if his mind was on his job for the rest of that afternoon, but thankfully I can't recall that there were any reported accidents!

Back in the office, I do remember that my filing system went all to pot and as you can imagine, I didn't check many more invoices for the rest of that day. My mind was far too busy drawing up its plan of action.

That night, as soon as I'd finished eating my tea, my fingers began itching to do something constructive. So with the key jingling in my pocket and my Mam's bucket dangling over my arm, off I went, stopping only once to visit the shop on the corner of our street. It's hard to believe that this was the same girl who would go to any lengths to avoid walking into a shop, let alone asking for something at a shop counter, yet here I was purchasing a bar of heavy green soap!

I must have looked a comical sight that evening, as I plodded through the quiet side streets, swinging my red plastic bucket, but I honestly didn't care what people were saying about me – I was on my way to my very first home.

It was an indescribable feeling, unlocking the front door of the house for the first time and stepping across its threshold. I honestly didn't know quite how or where to begin. I only knew that my hands needed to be doing something, so I began by weeping for joy, then I wiped my eyes, said a prayer of thanksgiving and eventually got around to boiling a kettle full of water. Into my red plastic bucket I plopped the scrubbing brush, the soap and the floor cloth and for some reason, a reason which I can't for the life of me understand, I made my way up the stairs and into the smaller of the two bedrooms.

Now is the time to tell you that I'd never done any dusting before, let alone tackled any filthy paint work – isn't that a terrible admission to make? But that night, as I looked around at the shabbiness of my new home, I knew that the responsibility for it's cleanliness was now all mine and I found myself thrilling at the prospect.

With a song on my lips, I began to scour the bottom sash of the window pane and I remember taking a step back, like the great artists do when they are about to admire their painting, and being tickled pink with the effect that I was making. And then, after taking a little gulp, I began to exert the same enthusiasm on the top sash, hoping that I'd be able to achieve the same transformation there.

You know what happened, don't you... The dirty sudsy water ran in thin grey rivulets down onto my gleaming white window frame and I laughed out loud at my naivety. That night, in the privacy of my own home, I learnt the first and last rule of spring cleaning – you must always start at the top.

As the weeks passed, John and I found that we possessed no great qualities when it came to DIY but although I say it myself, we excelled at being labourers. In fact it was often pointed out to me laughingly by my Dad, that I'd missed my vocation in life – because I had the makings of a wonderful 'gaffer'... One thing I did become a dab hand at though, was making pots of tea – not Earl Grey or Darjeeling you understand – just the sort of tea that sloshes down the back of your throat and washes away the powdery taste of plaster.

Before our very eyes, as the magicians say, our little house began to take shape. Grimy fireplaces were vigorously levered out, dreary wallpaper was contentiously scrapped away and shovel loads of bricks and rubble were scooped up from every corner.

Dad, and the men that he knew, rallied round to help us. They gave of themselves with their skills, their energy and their stamina, and all we had to offer them in return was our heartfelt thanks – and of course gallons and gallons of strong sweet tea. But what is so unforgettable, is the spirit in which they helped us. No job seemed too daunting for them to tackle and every undertaking was done with a whistle and a smile.

On and on we all worked, some weeks seeming to make hardly any progress at all, but gradually Dad's strong willing hands, and those of his friends, transformed the dark and dingy rooms into a bright and cheerful home for us, and for the rest of our lives John and I will be grateful to them all for all of their hard work.

Now you know why this clumsy old key is so special to me. It takes me back to those early, happy days, when a smiling face was just around the corner. It's a symbol if you like, of my first tentative step towards independence. It's proof, that with help, support and a little understanding, disabled people such as myself, can witness small but perfect miracles in their lives – the things that able bodied people take for granted. We disabled people don't want to reach for the stars you know – we just want to reach out and touch the odd sunbeam...

Yesterday, the key in my hand had winked at me, as if trying to say, 'Keep on going, you're doing fine,' and feeling refreshed and invigorated I had tidied up the cupboard in the bedroom once more. The Hoover still loomed at my side but I just laughed at it and carried it back down the stairs again. The whole morning had been a complete and utter waste of time – or had it?

Dear Lord,

Thankyou for the cheerful folk of this world. For the people who, with their foresight and stamina have the ability to turn our simple dreams into blinding reality.

Bless our homes Lord, however small and humble they may be, and make us aware of our good fortune every time we hold in our hands, our own front door key.

Embrace the homeless of this world Lord, cushion them with kindness, and who knows, perhaps one day, they too will be granted a welcoming hearth and a comfortable place to rest. Amen.

THE SAFE HAVEN

I have this strange obsession with shoes. No, obsession isn't really the right word – it's more a fascination. I just love admiring and delighting in other people's footwear.

I can't say exactly when this fixation began, just recently I think, but lately I find that whenever I go into town to do my weekly shopping, I'm spending more and more time either gazing wistfully into the windows of the shoe shops, or else I'm zooming my way through some superstore, searching excitedly for its shoe department.

And I hadn't realised until recently just how exquisitely some shoes are made, or in fact how expensive they can be, but my, some look really stylish!

I suppose this infatuation of mine stems from a tiny bit of jealousy on my part because all my life I've been able to wear only 'flatties', when in truth I would give almost anything to be able to step out in a pair of elegant high heels.

I remember in my younger days, how I was often tempted to buy myself a pair of fashionable shoes and I can see myself now, behaving like some eager Cinderella, struggling to induce my feet into a pair of totally unsuitable shoes. I'd go teetering and tottering around shoe racks, grabbing hold of anything and anyone who happened to be at hand, and whoever had been there with me at the time used to laughingly shake their heads and tell me to stick to the shoes that felt safe and comfortable. Time and time again I would concede miserably to their advice but this has never stopped me from drooling over footwear in the way that some ladies drool over jewellery.

Folk must think I'm a bit loopy when they see me staring at the ground because no matter where I am, whether I'm sitting in a ballroom or sitting on a promenade, my eyes are eventually drawn down towards people's feet.

I've seen people wearing shoes that were encrusted in silver stars and I've seen others wearing stilettos that were studded with diamante. I've seen toe-less sandals with gold leaf patterns snaking around their heels and I've seen sling back slippers, designed in the most sumptuous materials. Such variety, such extravagance, such elegance... And then I've looked down at my own frumpy footwear and sighed with resignation.

Just for the fun of it, why don't you and I kick off our walking boots and change into some really snazzy party shoes. We'll forget about our corns and bunions for a little while as we sashay down this final road together - a road which will eventually lead us to a safe haven.

From the moment I stepped into my shimmering white wedding gown and my white satin shoes, I knew exactly how an actress must feel when she dons the costume of the character that she is about to portray. It was as if something magical happened to me and for the first time in my life I felt truly beautiful. Sheer happiness seemed to transfigure my irregular features or was it simply that I was tasting at last, that overpowering feeling of contentment. A contentment which came from knowing that John was waiting in the chapel —waiting only for me.

Even now when strangers ask me, 'Is your husband disabled too?' my back immediately straightens and I must admit to a small serge of defiance when I tell them, "No!" Sometimes I'm even tempted to give them a silly reply, such as, 'He's a trapeze artist or an all-in wrestler,' but instead of voicing any of these absurdities I just suppress a little giggle.

I gave up a long time ago trying to figure out just why John chose me – why do any of us choose our partners? Instinct I guess! There's nothing strange or astonishing about our partnership. It's like a black person who's in love with a white person.... I can't see that there's anything unusual about that either. Undoubtedly the problems are there, but none that can't be resolved by two intelligent people, who, if left to their own devices, can endeavour to work things out together. It's people's prejudices that I find difficult to understand – the loving part comes easy.

Speaking of love, I thought that now would be a good time to tell you a little bit about our wedding day. Not that I can remember a great deal about it, but like extracts from my favourite movie, there are certain scenes that will stay in my memory forever.

I can remember the beginning of the day – how I awoke to the sound of torrential rain – and I can remember the end of the day – laying safe and secure in John's arms – but the bits in between are a complete hotchpotch of moments, moments which, when put together, somehow make up a very special occasion.

Looking back I'm sure that Mam and Dad could have come up with a hundred plausible reasons why our marriage couldn't possibly work but thankfully they kept all these reasons to themselves. Maybe when they saw the joy magnified in our faces they simply hadn't the heart to dash our expectations? Who knows what they were thinking and saying to one another in their most private of moments but not one whisper of doubt ever crossed their lips as the weeks and months slipped busily by.

Since our engagement Mam had squirrel-like stowing away all sorts of foodstuffs in the bottom of her wardrobe. Icing sugar, flour, dried fruit…you name it, it was there. My Nana and my three Great Aunts were to cater for our reception and John and I were more than happy to leave everything in their capable hands. Baking was second nature to them all, so we knew at least that the wedding breakfast would be perfect. The taxi – I wasn't so sure about!

Now some girls have a Rolls Royce to take them to the church to get married and others have a horse and carriage, but me, I had something quite different – I had a taxi that doubled as a funeral car – and between me and you I think the driver had his dates a bit mixed up because Dad and I were driven the short distance to the chapel at a very slow pace. In fact the only thing missing that morning was a sober faced man in a tall black hat, walking with dignity in front of the car. Honestly, we laughed all the way to the church, it was hilarious.

Miraculously the teeming rain had ceased just before leaving the house but I can still remember having to concentrate really hard in order to keep my dress from trailing into the puddles which glittered on the pavement – juggling at the same time with my small pretty bouquet – a trivial affair of tiny red rosebuds. At least this distracted me from the small crowd of people who had gathered outside the chapel to wish John and I good luck.

Somehow I survived the sea of faces and at last I was inside the chapel porch, where through the open double doors I could see our waiting guests. A hundred and twenty people turned to face us as the mellow tones of the organ announced our arrival and I'm sure that if those guests were truthful they would admit that deep, deep in their hearts that they had never expected me to marry. Yet here I was, without any hesitation, walking slowly and shyly towards John.

His was the face that I searched for and when our eyes met, he smiled. It wasn't the smile of regret, it was a smile which said, 'Come on Lynda, let's get this blinking show on the road....'

Now it's my turn to be honest with you – I too hadn't expected that someone as wonderful as John would one day come along. Of course I had hoped and had prayed that he would, but I hadn't really expected it to happen. No, the whole affair had taken me completely by surprise.

I can't say that I've ever felt grateful to John for marrying me, I've always known my worth, but as I joined him at the communion rail, that January morning, I couldn't help but give thanks to the Lord for our meeting.

We were allowed to say our wedding vows simultaneously to save me any undue embarrassment and the clearest, most overwhelming memory I have of that day, is of John and I kneeling side by side at the alter rail with the Minister's hands clasped firmly round our shoulders. There was strength in those arms, which is impossible for me to describe. It was as if they were willing us to stay together – cementing us together – and the minister's loud booming voice carried with it a conviction that defied us never ever to part. There's no doubt in my mind that there was a presence in the chapel that morning – a spirit that poured muted blessings over our union.

Whenever I think back to our wedding day, it isn't only John's face that I see, I see the faces of the people who shared that day with us. People who had genuinely cared and feared for our future... They had no need to be fearful, John and I both knew that we could make one another happy. Yet never in our wildest moments did we ever imagine the joy that the future held in store...?

How could I ever forget Dad's speech! A speech which never actually got off the ground because of the tears which came so unexpectedly – tears which were so out of character for my jovial, forthright father.

I remember also, the stream of cars that escorted John and I through the lashing rain to the railway station. Each car crammed with mischievous, grinning faces – intent on making our departure into the City as memorable as possible. Good wishes were on the lips of everyone and they floated through the air like clouds of invisible confetti.

It had all seemed so easy then – the happy ever after part - I wasn't aware that I was crossing a threshold and entering into a world where my faith and my physical capabilities were going to be stretched to their upper limits.

How much easier life would have been had I chosen to remain single and to stay at home with my Mam and Dad? For instance, there would have been no worries to keep me awake at night, no stressful decisions to be made. There would have been no cooking or house-work to exhaust me... But neither would there have been any great achievements! There would have been no cuddles in the darkness - no baby kisses!

As I write this chapter I'm actually looking at a photograph of John and I, taken on the day of our wedding. My how we've changed. I hardly recognise the two young people who are laughing so self-consciously into the camera. We were two naïve youngsters, looking into a future with eyes that couldn't see past our wedding day.

I even had a waistline then. And there's no grey in my hair, no lines on my face, as there are today – lines borne of laughing and living. That young body hadn't known any real pain in those days and those soft smooth hands hadn't known any hard work.

Only my heart it seems, has remained the same. It's a bit battered and bruised perhaps, with shedding too many tears, but it's a tender heart still. A heart that's always seeking out goodness and recognising sincerity in others... It's a heart that's still bursting with happiness...

At weddings these days, the young people take video recordings to help them to remember their 'Big Day'. I had no need to…I have only to peep inside an old dusty shoe box and see once again my pair of white satin shoes...(flat ones of course.) And anyway, I doubt if any video recorder could have captured the warm glow of love that was burning within me, on that January morning more than thirty years ago…. How do I remember the feeling? That's easy – I still feel the same tingle today.

Let's kneel and say our last prayer together.

Dear Lord,

Thank You for bringing us this far and for plotting our route in such a thoughtful and generous way. By giving us this safe haven You have indeed given us a comfortable and homely place to rest, and when the time is right Lord, You and You alone will give us the courage to journey on.

Stay close beside us Lord; don't ever leave us, because during the next lap of our journey we're going to need Your love and Your reassuring presence more than we've ever needed them before. Amen.

Our Wedding Day